LET'S TAKE THE KIDS TO LONDON

A FAMILY TRAVEL GUIDE

David S. White

Writers Club Press

New York Lincoln Shanghai

Let's Take the Kids to London
A Family Travel Guide

Writers Club Press
an imprint of iUniverse, Inc.

iUniverse books may be ordered through booksellers or by contacting:

iUniverse
2021 Pine Lake Road, Suite 100
Lincoln, NE 68512
www.iuniverse.com
1-800-Authors (1-800-288-4677)

The views expressed in this work are solely those of the author and do not necessarily reflect the views of the publisher, and the publisher hereby disclaims any responsibility for them.

This edition of *Let's Take the Kids to London* was updated in 2007. For more information about family travel to London, please see our website at www.KidsToLondon.com

ISBN-13: 978-0-595-13953-8
ISBN-10: 0-595-13953-1

Printed in the United States of America

Let's Take the Kids to London

To Deb, Daniel and Laura—a family that shares its love of travel, books, and each other.

Contents

Introduction To The Revised Edition

Time Flies

> "How did it get so late so soon? It's night before it's afternoon. December is here before it's June. My goodness how the time has flewn. How did it get so late so soon?"
>
> —Theodor Seuss Geisel

It has been more than ten years since our first family trip to London. Ten years is a blink of the eye in the history of the city, but there have been significant changes even during that short period. In revising *Let's Take the Kids to London* we've included updated information on the city's enduring tourist attractions and added descriptions of new sights and activities for families traveling to London.

We realize that some change is almost constant—opening hours and admission prices change almost as quickly as London's fickle weather. And some change is almost negligible—the Ceremony of the Keys at the Tower of London is virtually unaltered over hundreds of years.

This updated book is like a roadmap. It was carefully developed and was correct when printed. But a wise traveler checks local road conditions before each trip. The internet is one way to stay current and we have included website addresses for most of the sights described in our text (of course, web addresses are also subject to change). We also post updates and new information on the *Let's Take the Kids to London* website. Visit us at www.KidsToLondon.com.

A Method To Our Madness

Many travel books put the practical before the poetic. They describe what to pack, where to stay, and when to go before describing all the wonderful things to see and do at your destination. We've decided to flip-flop the order of the traditional travel book and let you read our book this way:

- First, learn something about London's great family activities and its fantastic palaces, parks, theaters, cathedrals, and museums—the things you want to see and do.
- Then browse through an extensive section on planning, where to stay, and other tips we have learned (sometimes the hard way) after many trips to London with our kids.

With this premise, we'll only delay a couple of paragraphs for introductions. There is a reason why the title of this book is *Let's Take the Kids to London*. That phrase is exactly what we said when our family of four took its first, serendipitous trip to Britain. From that experience, the trips that followed, and many hours of additional research, we converted the phrase into the book.

Will our observations be useful to you? No two people see London the same way, but here is our perspective. We have traveled to London with children of different ages and sexes: a 6-year-old boy, a 10-year-old girl, an 11-year-old boy, a 12-year-old girl, an 8-year-old boy, and a 15-year-old girl. They're the same two children—our son and daughter—but they have grown and experienced London differently over the years. Of course, during this same period their parents have not gotten any older (just wiser).

How To Read This Book

With a cup of tea, feet propped up, kids put to bed. Initial planning for a trip is a time for dreaming. We will paint a picture of London, you imagine your family in the picture. As imagination turns to serious consideration, you'll need details on London's sights and activities. We have included sections called *Where? What? £?* throughout this book. This is our standard format to tell you:

- Where each sight is located
- How to get there (usually by the Underground or "Tube," London's subway)
- The exact address
- Phone numbers and email addresses for more information
- Hours the sight is open
- About how long you can expect to spend at the sight
- Admission cost ranges
- A website address for more information

A little more about how we have organized this book. We start with the prime tourist destinations in central London. After that, we explore up and down the River Thames. Next we cover family activities in and around London. Then we take a field trip to give you a taste of what lies outside of London in the English countryside. Finally, it's down to practical matters with some planning advice and travel tips we have learned along the way.

PART 1

Look Kids! It's ...

The Tower Of London

"I know where we're going," said Judy, as they turned a corner.
"It's the Tower of London!" exclaimed Jonathan.
Paddington had never been to the Tower of London before and
he was most impressed. It was much, much bigger than he had
pictured.

—from *Paddington at the Tower*
by Michael Bond and Fred Banbery

Will kids enjoy the Tower of London? You bet! In fact, if you only have
time to take your children to one historic spot in London, make it the
Tower. The Tower of London offers a virtual smorgasbord of English
history and culture within its ancient walls. Take your pick from this
partial menu:

- Beauty—the crown jewels
- Tragedy—dismal dungeons and prison cells galore
- Legend—captive ravens and wandering ghosts
- Horror—beheadings on the Tower Green
- Tradition—the ancient Ceremony of the Keys

The Tower's tour guides—Yeoman Warders—are informative and
friendly and most of them make a special effort to peak the interests of
young visitors. A tour with a Yeoman Warder may be the "crown jewel" of

your Tower visit because the Warders provide an insider's perspective that is every bit as memorable as the real crown jewels displayed in the Tower.

Please don't call them Beefeaters; these are Yeoman Warders, retired career members of the British military. The Tower of London is their home and many of the 36 Warders and their families live on the grounds of the Tower. You have to look closely to spot the domestic mixed in with the historic, but you may see children's play equipment, a pet cat, hanging laundry and other evidence of the residents' private lives. The Tower forms a walled village within the city of London, but you won't see the private pub or family housing on the public tour. One stop on the Tower tour where you may get a sense of this community is the Chapel of St. Peter ad Vincula. While this is a royal chapel and historic site, it is also the community church for Tower residents. The Royal Family worships here on occasion, but this is also where Yeoman Warders' grandchildren may be baptized.

William the Conqueror began building the Tower in 1078, shortly after taking over England. It was his way of letting the natives know that London was under new management. For perspective, ask your children if they can name any place in North America that was built in 1078. Not Williamsburg, not New York, not St. Augustine, not the Pilgrim settlements. They'll get the idea—the Tower of London is *old*. The Tower was expanded over hundreds of years to become the fortress you see today. It has served as prison, palace, zoo, armory, execution spot, place of worship, and tourist attraction.

As a tourist destination, one of the Tower's most popular exhibits is the crown jewels. The jewels are beautifully displayed and while the lines to see the jewels may be long, they are well managed. Based on advice from the Disney organization, Tower management added several multi-screen videos and other introductory displays to reduce the boredom of waiting in line to see the jewels. Fortunately, the Tower did not further "Disneyfy" the jewel displays. There is no *Pirates of the Jewel Mountain* ride here, just a moving walkway which inches visitors past the jewel cases and makes sure that no one lingers too long.

Children may find the security precautions in the Jewel House to be almost as impressive as the jewels themselves. The massive doors leave no doubt that you are essentially walking through a very large bank vault to view the jewels. The high tech, high security Jewel House is a far cry from the way the jewels were first displayed at the Tower. During the 1600s the crown jewels were simply locked in a cabinet. To see the jewels, visitors just asked the custodian and paid a small fee! Not surprisingly, an attempt was made to steal the crown jewels during this period, but luckily the thieves were caught making their getaway. Security was tightened, repeatedly, and the jewels have been safely guarded ever since.

The central White Tower contains displays of ancient armor and weapons including Tudor and Stuart royal armor, weapons from the reign of Henry VIII, and British war trophies. Kids will be drawn to the child-sized armor worn by young princes and to the equine armor that protected royal horses almost as well as royal riders.

The Tower Green was the site of several notorious executions—King Henry VIII had a frequent chopper account here—but for all its association with beheadings and imprisonment, there's very little of the macabre at the Tower today. Leave that to the plastic-gore folks at the London Dungeon or Madame Tussaud's Wax Museum. The Tower's Yeoman Warders spin a few sinister stories of Tower executions that elicit "eews" and "yucks" from children in the audience, but the Warders are so good-natured that a visit to the Tower is appropriate for all ages.

Sir Walter Raleigh was one famous Tower prisoner who is familiar to many Americans. Imprisoned here three times, Sir Walter made himself quite comfortable in the Tower. His family moved in with him and brought along furniture, books and other comforts of home. But—and this is a big "but"—Sir Walter was executed after his third stay in the Tower. He lost his head elsewhere in London, not on Tower Green.

Today the Tower's only prisoners are a flock of birds. During their visit, children will undoubtedly hear the legend: if the ravens leave the Tower of London, the town is toast! Actually, that's not exactly the legend, but it does explain why the birds' wings are clipped. The legend really says that if the ravens leave, the White Tower will crumble and a disaster will befall England.

The national importance of the ravens was demonstrated during an unfortunate incident at the Tower of London. While preparing for a visit by the Royal Family, a police dog sniffed through the Tower grounds searching for possible bombs. During his search, Charlie the bomb dog was pecked by Charlie the raven. A former bird-hunting dog, canine Charlie grabbed raven Charlie in his mouth. The raven struggled and the dog instinctively bit down, killing the bird. The British press had a field day, members of the public were outraged, and we suspect that the dog had to undergo counseling. But the Yeoman Warder who told us most of this story—minus the counseling comment—was nonplused: "Big deal, we can always get another raven," he admitted.

During summer months, thousands of tourists stream into the Tower of London. Plan to arrive at the Tower when it opens and head straight for the crown jewels to avoid long lines. You can buy a ticket in advance by telephone, on the Tower's website, from most London Underground stations and from many tour operators.

The Ceremony Of The Keys

Want to see a free and nearly private ceremony in the Tower of London? The Tower allows about 50 people to attend the nightly Ceremony of the Keys—the ancient and now ceremonial locking of the Tower gates. Attending the ceremony requires a little footwork. Send for a ticket as far in advance as possible (six months ahead is not too soon). Write to:

The Ceremony of the Keys Office
HM Tower of London
London

EC3N 4AB
United Kingdom

In your letter include the:

- Date you want to attend (provide at least two alternate dates)
- Number of people in your party (maximum is 6 from April through October and 15 during other months)
- Names and addresses of everyone who will attend

Send the letter along with a self-addressed envelope and two international postal reply coupons (available at U.S. post offices) to cover the return postage.

On the night of the ceremony, ticket holders are escorted into the Tower at 9:30 p.m., long after tourists have left. A Yeoman Warder explains the history of the solemn 700-year-old ceremonial locking of the Tower's gates. After a brief introduction, visitors line up near the Bloody Tower gate to watch the Tower of London's very real military guard unit escort the Chief Warder as he locks the Tower. In modern times, the Ceremony of the Keys is largely symbolic, but to understand how important this ceremony still is, consider what we experienced the first time we attended.

It was the night of the 100th anniversary celebration for nearby Tower Bridge. Bands were playing just outside the Tower of London's walls, but arrangements had been made to stop the music during the Ceremony of the Keys. The ceremony has been going on every night for the past 700 years and *nothing* stops it. At the appointed hour visitors gathered inside the Tower, the guards were about to begin the ceremony, yet the band outside kept playing. The Yeoman Warder looked at his watch, frowned, looked again, but there was still no break in the music. At this point the Warder's supervisor showed up, spoke into his walkie-talkie, and made a pointed comment about "putting a stop to this nonsense." He ran off, and a minute or so later, the band abruptly stopped in mid-song. Maybe it was coincidence, or maybe the band-leader was reminded of the number of executions carried out just a few hundred feet away on the Tower grounds! The 700-year-old Ceremony of the Keys went on, while the 100-year-young Tower Bridge celebration took a short break.

On another evening at the Tower of London we learned that it is not just the Yeoman Warders who take the ceremony seriously. Different British military units rotate guard duty at the Tower. On this visit the guards were Gurkhas, elite British Army troops from Nepal. During the ceremony, the guards' commands were issued in crisp, loud, but heavily accented English. It was the same ceremony as performed by regular British troops, but visitors almost needed subtitles to understand it. After the ceremony, a Yeoman Warder explained that the Gurkhas take guarding the Tower very seriously and very literally. One Christmas Eve, the standing order for the guard was that all visitors had to leave the Tower immediately after attending the chapel service. The Gurkha guards escorted *everyone* from the church out of the Tower—no exceptions—including family members of Yeoman Warders who live on the grounds. The exiled family members had to phone friends at home inside the Tower to get back into their own homes on Christmas Eve! The Gurkha guards certainly secured the Tower, but you wonder if they would have allowed even Santa Claus in that night!

Here are a few practical hints for visitors attending the Ceremony of the Keys. Arrive early. If possible, stay in the front of the tour group and stand directly opposite the gate to the Bloody Tower. When signaled by the Yeoman Warder, move quickly through the gate to see the completion of the ceremony in the inner courtyard. The Yeoman Warders ask that visitors not talk during the ceremony. Silence is more than a mark of respect—half the fun of the ceremony is listening to the sounds: the guards' synchronous footsteps on the cobblestones, the jangling keys, the shouted commands, the bugler's notes.

One other important issue, especially for visitors with children, is that the Tower's restroom facilities are not open before, during or after the Ceremony of the Keys. The following is a true story; the names have been omitted to protect the easily embarrassed.

Hearing the first footfalls of the guards, the father peered down the pathway toward the gate of the Byward Tower. "Dad. Dad!" whispered a small, urgent voice. "I have to go the bathroom." Hoping against the inevitable, the father replied: "Can't you wait, son? The bathrooms are all closed." But alas, as every parent knows, when a child has to go, he *has* to go, even in the Tower of London. Fortunately, a sympathetic Yeoman Warder earned the father's enduring gratitude. "Bring the little fellow this way," he offered, and led the pair through a gate toward the White Tower. "Let him use the wall, it's seen worse," said the ever-practical Warder. The crisis was resolved, but the father missed the start of the ceremony. We have it on good authority that he and his son returned to the Tower the following year to see the entire Ceremony of the Keys. This time, they planned ahead and used the public restroom just outside the Tower gates *before* the ceremony.

Tower Chapel Services And Special Events

Restroom emergencies aside, there is one other way you can glimpse more of the Tower than the average tourist. If you are truly interested, ask a Yeoman Warder about attending church services in the Tower's Chapel Royal of St. Peter ad Vincula. Services are usually at 11:00 a.m. and 3:30 p.m. on Sunday and at 8:00 a.m. and 5:00 p.m. during the week. Remember, this not a tourist event, it is a real worship service for people who live in the Tower. Go with respect.

Special events abound at the Tower, especially on weekends in the summer, during school breaks, and around major holidays. It is always worthwhile checking the Historic Royal Palaces website (www.hrp.org.uk) for information on upcoming events. One such event that it is hard to ignore are gun salutes at the Tower. For royal occasions, like the Monarch's birthday, a simple 21 gun salute just won't do. The Tower fires off a 62 gun salute: the traditional 21 gun salute, plus 20 because the Tower is a royal palace and fortress and an extra 21 as a mark of respect for the sovereign from the City of London. Since the end of the Second World War gun salutes have been fired from four 25-pound guns on Tower Wharf by the Honourable Artillery Company, the oldest armed body in Britain.

An ambitious plan has improved landscaping, ticketing facilities, pedestrian walkways, river piers, and other areas in the Tower Hill neighborhood surrounding the Tower. With buildings and fortifications that are almost 1,000 years old, archeological and restoration work is an ongoing endeavor at the Tower of London. Some of these projects literally unearth "new" information about the Tower's history, making the Tower more than a static historical site.

Tower Bridge

Tower Bridge ties with Big Ben as the most recognizable landmark in London. Don't make the novice tourist's mistake of referring to Tower Bridge as London Bridge, its nondescript neighbor located a mile upstream. Despite the famous children's song, London Bridge is now just a modern bridge in a historic location on the River Thames. Tower Bridge, on the other hand, deserves a visit.

A tour shows the inner workings of the bridge and explains how the span was opened in Victorian times by huge steam engines. Kids can experiment with operating models and interactive computers that detail the drawbridge's engineering principles. Technically speaking, Tower Bridge is a *bascule* bridge, from the French word for see-saw. Undoubtedly this is the largest see-saw in London. Once outside the engine rooms, take in the great views from the top of the bridge, 140 feet above. Don't worry, you're in an enclosed walkway so nobody is going to fall off. The walkways were designed so that pedestrians could still walk across when the drawspan was raised, but this required detouring up and down long stairways and the walkways were closed not long after the bridge was built. The re-opened walkways finally gained popularity as a tourist attraction.

If you want to forego the museum and enclosed walkway, there is no charge to walk across the bridge itself. This is a prime spot to take a picture of the family, so set up the shot to get the Tower of London in the background. While you are there maybe a ship will come along and the bridge will be raised. Bridge openings are rare these days since London is not the seagoing city it once was. But there is no shortage of traffic *on* the bridge with nearly 150,000 cars, trucks, and buses crossing this important London link every day.

*　　　　　*　　　　　*

Where? When? £?

Tower of London

Location	On the north bank of the Thames, downstream (east) of central London
Tube	Tower Hill station (Circle and District lines)
Address	Tower of London, Tower Hill, EC3N 4AB
Phone	Information line: 0870 756 6060 Chapel service information: 0870 751 5177 Telephone ticket sales: 0870 756 7070
Hours	In March through October the Tower is open from 9:00 a.m. to 6:00 p.m. Monday through Saturday. On Sunday, the hours are 10:00 a.m. to 6:00 p.m. The rest of the year, hours are 9:00 a.m. to 5:00 p.m. on Tuesday through Saturday and 10:00 a.m. to 5:00 p.m. on Sunday and Monday. Buildings close 30 minutes after last admission; grounds close 30 minutes later. The Tower is closed December 24-26 and January 1. Yeoman Warder Tours start at 9:30 a.m. (Sundays 10:00 a.m.), then every 30 minutes until 3:30 p.m. (2:30 in winter). These tours last about an hour.
Time Required	Three hours

Tower of London

Admission	Visiting the Tower of London is expensive but worthwhile. Getting tickets in advance avoids waiting in long lines. Buy tickets at the Tower, at any London Underground station, online or by phone. There are discounts for families, students, and seniors. Combination tickets are also available covering Tower of London and Hampton Court Palace.
Facilities	Armouries cafeteria inside Tower grounds, café and snack bars on nearby Wharf and along Great Tower Street. No outside food allowed in restaurant or café—no formal outdoor picnic areas, but visitors may bring food and sit on benches on the Tower's grounds. Toilets and baby-changing area in the Brick Tower. Many areas of the Tower are not wheelchair accessible.
Website	www.hrp.org.uk

Where? When? £?

Tower Bridge Exhibition

Location	Crosses the Thames at the Tower of London. Enter the exhibit and walkway on the northwest side of the bridge, closest to the Tower, through a glass-enclosed ticket booth and lobby.
Tube	London Bridge station (Northern line) or Tower Hill station (Circle and District lines)
Address	The Tower Bridge Exhibition, Tower Bridge, London SE1 2UP
Phone	020 7403 3761
Hours	In April through September the Exhibition is open from 10:00 a.m. to 6:30 p.m. In October through March, the hours are 9:30 a.m. to 6:00 p.m. Last entry is one hour before closing. Closed December 24-25.
Time Required	60 to 90 minutes
Admission	Ticket prices are moderate and can be purchased at the Bridge or online. There are discounts for families, students, and seniors. Children under age five get in free.
Facilities	Toilets and baby-changing areas. All areas are wheelchair accessible.
Website	www.towerbridge.org.uk

Buckingham Palace

'By gumdrops!' whispered the Big Friendly Giant. 'Is this really it?'

'There's the Palace,' Sophie whispered back.

Not more than a hundred yards away, through the tall trees in the garden, across the mown lawn and the tidy flower-beds, the massive shape of the Palace itself loomed through the darkness. It was made of whitish stone. The sheer size of it staggered the BFG.

—from *The BFG* by Roald Dahl

Although the Big Friendly Giant was impressed, Buckingham Palace is by no means the grandest palace in England. But like the White House in Washington, the grandeur of Buckingham Palace does not come strictly from architecture, but rather from its aura of tradition, ceremony, and power.

Originally to help defray the costs of restoring Windsor Castle, in recent years the Royal Family has allowed the public to peek inside Buckingham Palace. Just a peek, mind you, and only for a few weeks each year while the Royals are on vacation. Under this arrangement, Buckingham Palace State Rooms are usually open daily during August and September. Because tourists are admitted at timed intervals, the lines are reasonable and the Palace is not overly crowded. Security is tight, but visitors have plenty of time to stroll though the Palace's ornate rooms.

Seeing the inside of Buckingham Palace is not just a novelty for foreign tourists. A fair number of British citizens take the tour and finally get to see the inside of a place which has played an important, if ceremonial, role in their nation's history. During one August visit we over-heard a British mother telling her two daughters, "This is the piano where the young princesses Elizabeth and Margaret took their lessons when *they* were little girls." We will never know if this was impressive enough to inspire the visiting children to practice their piano lessons, but the mother deserves credit for trying.

Arriving at the Buckingham Palace Throne Room, a visiting child expressed disappointment: "That's the throne? It's just an old red chair!" Another looked around at the few side chairs and wondered where the royal princes sit when they come to visit.

At the end of the Buckingham Place tour, visitors stroll through parts of the Palace's 39-acre private garden. As the tour ends, there is an opportunity to browse the Palace gift shop filled with tasteful, but expensive mementos of your visit.

When the summer open house is over, tourists are reduced to gawk-ing at Buckingham Palace through a tall black iron fence. Invariably someone (usually a child) asks "Is anybody home?" For an answer, take a look at the roof. If the Royal Standard—the flag with a lion on it—is flying, the Sovereign is in residence. Historically, no flag flew above the Palace at other times, but now the Union Jack flies at Buckingham when the Royals are away from home.

By the way, when you peer through the fence you're actually looking at the back of Buckingham Palace. The front of the palace overlooks the private gardens—these are located in what seems to be the back yard to us common fence gawkers.

There are several other tourist sights associated with the Palace:

- The Royal Mews
- Clarence House

- Wellington Arch
- The Queen's Gallery

For a slightly better peek into the Royal backyard, especially the Royal tennis courts, visitors can climb to the top of nearby Wellington Arch. Once home to London's smallest police station, English Heritage restored and reopened the arch in 2001. Climbing atop Wellington Arch and spying on the Palace will entice many children, but the Royal art collection at the Gallery and Clarence House, home of the late Queen Mother, are of limited interest to kids. The Mews, site of the Royal stables and carriage house, is another matter.

The Royal Mews—I'll Take Falconry For $200, Alex ...

Why would a horse stable be called a "mews?" Originally, this was the home of the Royal falcons, and mewing referred to the shedding of the birds' feathers. Today the Mews is the headquarters of the Crown Equerry—the motor pool for the Royal Family. (But doesn't "Crown Equerry" sound so much better than "motor pool?") This is where the Royal Family's ceremonial coaches, limos, and horses are housed.

The Royal Family owns over 100 coaches and carriages and some of the most ornate are on display in the Royal Mews. For sheer opulence, check out the Gold State Coach. As the name implies, this coach is so heavily gold gilded it's a wonder that the Royal horses can even pull it. This golden fairy tale coach has been used at every coronation since 1821. Slightly lower on the opulence scale is the Irish State Coach, used at the annual opening of Parliament, and the Glass Coach that transported Lady Diana Spencer to St. Paul's Cathedral to begin her star-crossed marriage to Prince Charles.

Children touring the Royal Mews may quickly conclude that once you've seen one golden coach, you've seen them all. Let's see the horses! Since the Royal Family lives in luxury at Buckingham Palace, it's hardly a surprise that the Royal horses' quarters are none too shabby either. It doesn't even *smell* like a stable. The Cleveland Bay and Windsor Grey horses live in clean, bright stalls with tiled walls and each animal's name is displayed on a prominent placard. During a visit to the Royal Mews, our daughter Laura was surprised to find she shared a name with one of the horses. To her this was a dubious honor—she would have rather met a royal prince than a royal horse.

The Royal Mews is also the Royal Garage, home to a fleet of Royal motor cars. The Mews has converted a number of limos to run on liquid petroleum gas as the Royal Family's contribution to reducing London's air pollution. But the official in charge of the Mews has the title Master of the Queen's Horses, not Master of the Queen's Rolls Royces, and it is horses and carriages that most tourists come to see. The Mews is an agreeable attraction for most children, but if you are traveling with a young equestrian, the Mews is a "must see."

Like the Tower of London, the Royal Mews is a historic sight that also serves as a home to some of the people who work there, so make sure your children look for the domestic touches during their visit.

Clarence House

No one lives forever, but before her death at age 101, Elizabeth, the Queen Mother was truly pushing the longevity envelope. Clarence House was her home from 1953 to 2002. Her grandson, Prince Charles, then moved into Clarence House and did a bit of redecorating. Like Buckingham Palace, Clarence House is open to the public for a period during the summer. Clarence House is not a grand palace and the tour includes just a handful of official rooms on the ground floor of the building. There is little to interest children here, but the tour is relatively short.

Wellington Arch

Except during the annual summer opening, the gates to Buckingham Palace are closed to the public. But you can still sneak a peak into the Palace grounds from Wellington Arch, overlooking the backyard of Buckingham Palace near Hyde Park Corner. Tourists can climb to the top of the arch and peer into the gardens behind the palace. Wellington Arch was built as a grand gateway to the Palace and served many roles over the years, including playing host to London's smallest police station. The arch was restored by the English Heritage preservation organization as part of Britain's Millennium celebration.

The Queen's Gallery

If you're in London at a time when Buckingham Palace is not open, a visit to the Queen's Gallery provides a bit of the flavor of the palace through an extensive display of Royal artwork and furnishings. For the typical child visitor, though, the Queen's Gallery is going to prove a test of patience.

The Royal Treatment

In recent years, the institution of the Royal Family has undergone intense scrutiny. Consequently, you may run into Londoners who are strongly pro-royal, anti-royal, or who plainly don't care. Tourists generally have royal sights on their agendas and they want to know such royal trivia as "Is the Royal Family at Buckingham Palace or Windsor this week?" We asked a hotel desk clerk just this question on one trip to London and got a rather chilly response. "I don't follow the Royals, so I wouldn't know," was her reply. Excuse us for asking!

* * *

Where? When? £?

Buckingham Palace—The Tour

Location	At the west end of the Mall, bordered by Hyde, Green, and St. James's Parks. Ticket office is in Green Park, just across the street from the Palace. Tours enter on the south side of the Palace on Buckingham Palace Road.
Tube	Green Park station (Jubilee, Victoria, or Piccadilly lines), St. James's Park station (Circle or District line), or Victoria station (Circle, District, or Victoria lines)
Address	Ticket Sales and Information Office, The Official Residences of The Queen, London SW1A 1AA
Phone/email	020 7766 7300 bookinginfo@royalcollection.org.uk
Hours	Generally August and September from 9:45 a.m. to 4:00 p.m. Hours subject to change.
Time Required	One to two hours
Admission	Tickets to the Palace are moderately expensive. Tickets can be ordered online or by telephone (with a booking fee) or they can be purchased at the ticket office, located just across the street in Green Park, on days when the Palace is open. Ticket office opens at 9:30 a.m. There are discounts for families, students, and seniors. Children under age five get in free. Combined *Royal Day Out* tickets are available for the Palace, Queen's Gallery, and Royal Mews.

Buckingham Palace—The Tour

Facilities   Toilets are available at the end of the tour. Some areas of the Palace are not wheelchair accessible. Limited snack items are sold at the gift shop in the Palace's garden.

Website   www.royal.gov.uk
www.royalcollection.org.uk

Where? When? £?

Royal Mews

Location	A few hundred yards south of the Palace, where Buckingham Gate becomes Buckingham Palace Road
Tube	Victoria station (Circle, District, or Victoria lines)
Address	Ticket Sales and Information Office, The Official Residences of The Queen, London SW1A 1AA
Phone/email	020 7766 7300 bookinginfo@royalcollection.org.uk
Hours	The Mews is open from late March or early April through October. Normal hours are 11:00 a.m. to 4:00 p.m. When Buckingham Palace is open the hours for the Mews are 10:00 a.m. to 5:00 p.m. Last admission is 45 minutes before closing.
Time Required	An hour (more if you love horses and carriages)
Admission	Tickets are reasonably priced. Tickets can be ordered online or by telephone (with a booking fee) or they can be purchased at the Mews ticket office. There are discounts for families, students, and seniors. Children under age five get in free.
Facilities	Toilets and baby care rooms are available. The site is wheelchair accessible. No food available onsite.
Website	www.royal.gov.uk www.royalcollection.org.uk

Where? When? £?

Clarence House

Location	A few hundred yards east of Buckingham Palace, along The Mall, opposite St. James's Park
Tube	Green Park station (Jubilee, Victoria, or Piccadilly lines)
Phone/email	020 7766 7303
	bookinginfo@royalcollection.org.uk
Hours	Open daily from 10:00 a.m. to 5:30 p.m. during the summer opening, generally August through September. Last admission is one hour before closing.
Time Required	45 minutes to an hour
Admission	Tickets are reasonably priced. Tickets can be ordered online or by telephone (with a booking fee). There are discounts for children and those under age five get in free.
Facilities	The site tour is wheelchair accessible. No toilets or food available onsite.
Website	www.royal.gov.uk
	www.royalcollection.org.uk

Where? When? £?

Wellington Arch

Location	Hyde Park Corner, between Hyde Park and Buckingham Palace
Tube	Hyde Park Corner station (Piccadilly line)
Phone	020 7930 2726
Hours	Open Wednesday through Sunday from 10:00 a.m. to 5:00 p.m. Closes at 4:00 p.m. in November through March. Closed December 24-25 and January 1.
Time Required	30 minutes
Admission	Tickets are reasonably priced. There are discounts for children.
Facilities	The site is wheelchair accessible. No toilets or food available onsite.
Website	www.english-heritage.org.uk

Where? When? £?

The Queen's Gallery

Location	On the south side of Buckingham Palace on Buckingham Palace Road
Tube	Victoria station (Circle, District, or Victoria lines)
Address	Ticket Sales and Information Office, The Official Residences of The Queen, London SW1A 1AA
Phone/email	020 7766 7301 bookinginfo@royalcollection.org.uk
Hours	Open every day from 10:00 a.m. to 5:30 p.m. Last admission is one hour before closing. Closed December 25-26, Good Friday.
Time Required	One hour
Admission	Tickets are reasonably priced. Tickets can be ordered online or by telephone (with a booking fee). Limited ticket availability at the door. There are discounts for families, students, and seniors. Children under age five get in free.
Facilities	Toilets and baby care rooms are available. The site is wheelchair accessible. No food available onsite.
Website	www.royal.gov.uk www.royalcollection.org.uk

Old Dead Guys

Westminster Abbey

Touring cathedrals and churches may not rank high on your kids' sight-seeing priority list, but if there is one church in London for your family to see, it is Westminster Abbey. For adult visitors Westminster is a fascinating sight, drenched in history. Kings and queens from history books are more real when you come face-to-face with their final resting places and in Westminster Abbey this includes Henry III, Henry V, Queen Elizabeth I, and Mary Queen of Scots.

The Abbey estimates that about 3,300 other people are buried on the site! The role call also includes David Livingston, Isaac Newton, Charles Darwin, George Frederic Handel, and Laurence Olivier. At least one person, poet Ben Johnson, was buried standing upright and another, the infamous Oliver Cromwell, was only a temporary resident. Cromwell's body, along with those of several cohorts and family members, was removed by royal decree after King Charles II was restored to the throne in the mid-1600s. And the oldest of the interred is undeniably Thomas Parr, whose claim to fame was that he reportedly lived for more than 152 years before being buried in the Abbey in 1635.

But are so many "old dead guys" going to peak a child's interest? Not all of Westminster Abbey's history is ancient. Queen Elizabeth II was crowned here in 1953 and the Abbey was the site of Princess Diana's funeral in 1997 and the Queen Mother's funeral in 2002. The Abbey was also the location for a bit of action in *The Da Vinci Code*. The popular novel included scenes featuring Sir Isaac Newton's tomb and the

Chapter House in Westminster Abbey, but the Da Vinci Code movie was not filmed here. Westminster Abbey officials took a dim theological view of the story and refused entry to the filmmakers.

Recent history aside, Westminster Abbey is *old*. One of the first things William the Conqueror did after taking over England was to have himself crowned in the Norman abbey which stood on the site of Westminster Abbey. That was in 1066, over 900 years ago. Westminster Abbey was *re*built in 1245!

But again, is so much ancient history going to turn young visitors into reluctant tourists? There are ways to help prevent kids' eyes from glazing over while touring the Abbey. Have them look up as they enter Henry VII's Lady Chapel and they will find the banners and crests of the Knights of the Order of the Bath (the *clean* nights). If it isn't too crowded this is a good opportunity to take a moment, sit down, and study the variety of knights' shields—they form a virtual menagerie of animals, weaponry, peculiar symbols, colorful flags and coats of arms. Kids can pick out their favorites and speculate about some of the more unusual shields. Ask your children what their own shields would look like if they became Knights of the Order of the Bath.

A more modern historical tidbit which kids can search for in Westminster Abbey is a tiny hole in the wall at the back of the Lady Chapel. The hole was blasted out during the bombing of London in World War II. Fittingly, the hole is near one of the newer memorials in the Abbey—dedicated to Royal Air Force members who fought in the Battle of Britain. The tiny hole was the only appreciable war damage to the Abbey, despite being situated just a block from the tempting targets of Parliament and other government buildings. The Royal Air Force chapel window includes the crests from 68 fighter squadrons that defended Britain in 1940.

Then it's on to more old dead guys at Poet's Corner in the South Transept of the Abbey. Depending upon their ages, kids may recognize some of the famous poets, writers, and actors buried and memorialized in Poet's Corner. This impressive Dead Poets' Society includes Geoffrey Chaucer, Charles Dickens, Alfred Lord Tennyson, Robert Browning, and Rudyard Kipling.

Next stop is the cloisters, a covered square of corridors once used by the Abbey's monks and now filled with memorial plaques. The nearby Chapter House was the site of Parliament meetings in the 14th century. The College Garden is worth a look, although its hours differ from the Abbey's. During summer months, lunchtime concerts are sometimes held in the garden.

Not every monument or hidden mystery in Westminster Abbey is ancient or even mysterious. Observant visitors to the Abbey grounds can find one monument that official Abbey guidebooks generally ignore. Thomas Crapper—the unfortunately named plumber—was employed here in the late 1800s to install plumbing fixtures. Several manhole covers bearing the inscription T.CRAPPER & CO. remain today around Westminster Abbey.

Westminster Abbey is so overrun with tourists that it became difficult to hold religious services because of the noise of milling crowds. So the Abbey's Dean instituted a program to restore the calm of the sanctuary. This means controls on the size of tour groups and limits to the public tour route in Westminster Abbey. Instead of entering through the massive West Doors, tourists come through the North Doors just off Parliament Square. The tour route includes much of the Abbey, but it tries to reduce the flow of visitors walking around and through church services held in the central nave. Remember, you are not just visiting a historic site, but an active church where people come to worship and pray.

One final note. Despite its size, Westminster Abbey is not a cathedral, it is a "royal peculiar" (there's a joke here, but we will forgo it). The term means that the Abbey reports to the Monarch instead of the normal church hierarchy of bishops and archbishops. Technically, the Abbey is named The Collegiate Church of St Peter, Westminster, but don't try asking directions to the Abbey using that official moniker. Of course, it's no longer really an abbey since there are no monks in residence, but there once were, and the name has stuck.

St. Paul's Cathedral

> But at last they came to St. Paul's Cathedral, which was built a long time ago by a man with a bird's name. Wren it was … That is why so many birds live near Sir Christopher Wren's Cathedral, which also belongs to St. Paul, and that is why the Bird Woman lives there, too.

> —from *Mary Poppins* by P. L. Travers

Where is the religious center of old London? Westminster Abbey? St. Paul's Cathedral? The original St. Paul's burned down during the great fire of London in 1666, so the current cathedral is a relative newcomer compared to Westminster Abbey. Visiting children may note one effect of this newness—the old dead guys buried in St. Paul's are not as old, numerous, and famous as those buried in Westminster (they are just as dead, however). At this point in our narrative, we offer a blanket apology to the deceased and to any readers who are offended. In our defense, please remember that this is a book about kids as tourists and "old dead guys" is a realistic child's eye view of touring cathedrals and churches.

St. Paul's is a fitting monument to Sir Christopher Wren, London's greatest architect. Wren is buried here (yikes, another old dead guy) with the simple inscription *Si monumentum requiris circumspice*. If your Latin is rusty, we'll translate: "If you seek a monument, look around you." Other notables buried in St. Paul's include the Duke of Wellington and Admiral Lord Nelson. Gross-out note for kids: Nelson died at the battle of Trafalgar in 1805 and his body was placed in a keg of brandy for the long boat trip home. The same thing happened to American naval hero John Paul Jones, but with less success since sailors allegedly drank the brandy!

One of the features of the cathedral that fascinates children is the Whispering Gallery. You have to make a long climb to reach the gallery high inside the dome above the cathedral floor. When you catch your breath, turn and whisper against the circular wall. Your whisper can be heard by someone on the other side of the dome almost 130 feet away. While you're in the gallery, take a look at the cathedral's frescos. Climb even higher and you'll reach the Golden Gallery. This is a fantastic observation point from which you can see the entire city of London, but the climb is long and dizzying with almost 200 steps to the Whispering Gallery and a narrow 500 steps to the very top.

American visitors may be particularly interested in the American Memorial Chapel located behind the High Altar. This is a British tribute to 28,000 Americans who were based in Britain and lost their lives during World War II. A book containing the names of the war dead is displayed in the memorial.

Christopher Wren wanted to rebuild the entire city of London after the great fire of 1666 and he had even grander plans for St. Paul's Cathedral. It was not enough that the 360-foot high dome dominated the London skyline (it is still the second largest church dome in the world), Wren wanted the huge dome to be gilded with gold.

One feature remains from the pre-1666 cathedral. During the fire, a statue of poet John Donne supposedly crashed through the floor and landed in the crypt below. The statue was rescued and placed in the new cathedral. You can still see scorch marks on its base.

St. Paul's has been tested by fire throughout the ages and one of the enduring images of the present cathedral is a famous photograph of St. Paul's standing intact while the surrounding section of London burns during a World War II bombing raid. Children can read about the heroic men of the cathedral's fire watch who, instead of hiding in bomb shelters during the Blitz, risked their lives putting out fires in St. Paul's. Without them, it is unlikely that the cathedral would have survived.

St. Paul's, like Westminster Abbey, is both a historic site and a functioning church. While many may remember the funeral of Princess Diana in Westminster Abbey, St. Paul's was the site of Diana's wedding—a happier moment (or so it seemed at the time). Coronations are the purview of Westminster Abbey, but once enthroned, recent monarchs have celebrated birthdays and jubilees at St. Paul's.

St. Paul's is an active church and it is often closed to visitors for special worship services at unexpected times. During a visit to the cathedral, we were ushered out because of the arrival of hundreds of Girl Guides (the British Girl Scouts) attending a service to mark scouting's anniversary. While we didn't get to see much of St. Paul's that day, it was a great opportunity for our daughter, who was a Girl Scout at the time, to make another personal connection with England.

*　　　　　*　　　　　*

Where? When? £?

Westminster Abbey

Location	Just across the street from the Parliament building. Enter through the north doors next to Parliament Square.
Tube	Westminster station or St. James's Park station (both on Circle and District lines)
Address	Parliament Square, London SW1
Phone/email	020 7654 4900 info@westminster-abbey.org
Hours	Abbey: Monday Tuesday, Thursday and Friday from 9:30 a.m. to 4:45 p.m. On Wednesdays the Abbey is open until 7:00 p.m. and on Saturdays the Abbey is open from 9:30 a.m. to 2:45 p.m. Last admission is one hour before closing. Chapter House: 10:30 a.m. to 4:00 p.m. daily. Cloisters: 8:00 a.m. to 6:00 p.m. daily. Abbey Museum: 10:30 a.m. to 4:00 p.m. daily. College Garden: Tuesday, Wednesday and Thursday from 10:00 a.m. to 6:00 p.m. During October through March the garden closes at 4:00 p.m.
Time Required	One to three hours
Admission	Tickets are moderately priced. There are discounts for families, students, and seniors. Children under age 11 get in free. Admission to the Cloisters and College Garden is free. No charge for attending services.

Westminster Abbey

Facilities	Some areas are not wheelchair accessible. Toilets near west entrance. Coffee and snack carts on site.
Website	Abbey: www.westminster-abbey.org Chapter House: www.english-heritage.org.uk

Where? When? £?

St. Paul's Cathedral

Location	On Ludgate Hill, just north of the Thames, about halfway between Parliament and the Tower of London
Tube	St. Paul's station (Central line)
Address	St. Paul's Cathedral, The Chapter House, St. Paul's Churchyard, London EC4M 8AD
Phone/email	020 7246 8357 visits@stpaulscathedral.org.uk
Hours	Open for visitors Monday through Saturday from 8:30 a.m. to 5:00 p.m. Last admission at 4:00 p.m.
Time Required	One to two hours
Admission	Tickets are moderately priced. There are discounts for children, families, students, and seniors. Children under age seven get in free. Tickets can be purchased online.
Facilities	Café and restaurant (no outside food allowed). Toilets and baby-changing areas. Most areas are wheelchair accessible.
Website	www.stpauls.co.uk

Parliament and Big Ben

Children who are studying government in school *may* be interested in visiting Britain's Houses of Parliament—it's a long shot—but parents who really want to see Parliament can try selling the visit to their kids as a chance to peek inside the building where Big Ben is located.

Not to shatter any illusions, but Big Ben is not really Big Ben. This symbol of London is actually the clock tower of the Palace of Westminster and *Big Ben* simply refers to the bell inside the tower. That architectural fact hardly ever stops anyone from calling the tower Big Ben though. The origin of the nickname is not clear, but some claim that the clock was named after Sir Benjamin Hall, a construction supervisor during the installation of the tower. British residents can find out what makes Big Ben tick by requesting a clock tower tour from a Member of Parliament. Overseas visitors are excluded from tower touring due to security concerns.

While the Parliament building interiors are interesting, the historical trivia associated with the building can be equally fascinating. In the House of Commons chamber, visitors learn the origin of the expression "to toe the line." There is an actual line marked on the floor of the chamber and, no matter how vehement the debate, members who are speaking may not step across this line. The line is located so that opposing members are separated by more than a sword's length. In olden days, an angry member who drew his sword would not necessarily draw an opponent's blood. Disorderly conduct was (and sometimes still is) a problem in the chamber and the House of Commons' Sergeant-At-Arms has extraordinary powers to maintain the peace. The Sergeant has the authority to issue an arrest warrant for anyone in the country and have the unfortunate individual imprisoned for up to five years without possibility of appeal. You do not want to cross this guy, so toe the line!

Between the House of Commons and House of Lords the central dome's gold murals depict four saints representing the four sections of the United Kingdom: Saint David for Wales, Saint Patrick for Ireland, Saint Andrew for Scotland, and Saint George for England. Another impressive architectural feature of Parliament is the huge, medieval Westminster Hall. This is the oldest surviving piece of Westminster Palace, built in 1097. Unlike some restored old buildings, this place really looks like a medieval hall with its high hammerbeamed ceiling and dark, smoke-stained atmosphere. There are no ornate furnishings, no bright gold ornamentation, just the cold stonework and dark wood ceiling.

Because of security concerns, and the need to keep tourists from bothering the members while the legislature is in session, full access to Parliament is limited. British citizens can often get building passes through their MPs (Members of Parliament). Foreign visitors are not allowed to tour the buildings when Parliament is in session and over-seas tourist are limited to what were once called *Strangers Galleries* in both Houses of Parliament. Beginning in 2004, the visiting public was no longer referred to as *strangers* in Parliament. The galleries are now known as the Public Galleries. How democratic!

Understanding how best to tour Parliament is no simple task. Not too long after the Royal family started opening Buckingham Palace to summer visitors, Parliament began its own summer openings—usually held in August and September. This is the easiest way for an overseas visitor to tour Parliament. Tours are guided and last about 75 minutes.

Generally, Parliament is in session Monday through Thursday with lots of holiday breaks—politicians being the same on both sides of the Atlantic, they need plenty of time to schmooze with the electorate back home. The liveliest time to visit is during Question Time when members verbally parry and the opposition tries to zing the Prime Minister. Question Time is so popular that only British citizens stand a good chance at getting in. In theory, foreign visitors can be admitted to the House of Commons gallery with a *card of introduction* obtained from their London embassies. But, since each embassy only gets four cards per day, the odds are not good.

Tourists without advance tickets can also line up outside St. Stephen's entrance to Parliament, but a wait of one or two hours is common during the afternoons. Sometimes it is easier to get in during the late afternoon, early evening or a Friday. When Parliament is in session, there are separate lines for entering the House of Commons and the House of Lords. (Look up at the Parliament building—if the tower opposite Big Ben has a flag flying, Parliament is in session.) If nothing works, or if you get frustrated waiting in line, you can see an exhibit on the history of Parliament in the nearby 14th Century Jewel Tower, part of the old Palace of Westminster.

When all is said and done, the question remains: will kids enjoy a tour of Parliament? The answer is a definite maybe. There are no interactive exhibits here (thumbs down!), but no old dead guys either (thumbs up!).

Parliamentary Side Trips—In Search Of Abe Lincoln and Ben Franklin

It is a long way from a Kentucky log cabin to the London Borough of Westminster, but President Abraham Lincoln made the trip (at least in effigy). In Parliament Square, but closer to Westminster Abbey than Parliament, stands a statue of Honest Abe. This is hardly a major tourist attraction, but it makes an interesting footnote to your tour, and seeing Lincoln's statue is one way that American children can make a London connection to U.S. history. In fact, statues of famous Americans are fairly common in London. George Washington's statue is located in front of the National Gallery, Franklin Roosevelt and Winston Churchill share a park bench at the end of Grafton Street, and another statue of FDR is found in Grosvenor Square with a statue of Dwight Eisenhower nearby.

One famous American hero spent more time in London than Lincoln, Washington, Roosevelt, and Eisenhower combined. Benjamin Franklin lived for 18 years at a house on Craven Street, about a half a mile north of Parliament. Franklin—a Big Ben in his own time—performed a mixture of science and diplomacy from his London home. He beat a hasty retreat in 1775 just ahead of war between Britain and the American colonies.

After Franklin's departure, the house served as an anatomy school (specimens are on display), hotel, and office space. After falling into disrepair, the Benjamin Franklin House was restored in 2006 and opened to the public for interpretative tours and as an educational center. Visitors are taken on a sound-and-light tour through the house by a costumed guide who interacts with the recorded voices of Ben Franklin and other historical figures. The hands-on educational center offers children the chance to learn about Franklin's scientific contributions. The center is open to groups by appointment.

★   ★   ★

Where? When? £?

Parliament—Palace of Westminster

Location	Next to the Thames, in Westminster. Find Big Ben and you've found Parliament.
Tube	Westminster station (Circle and District lines)
Address	Information contacts: House of Commons Information Office, House of Commons, Westminster, London, SW1A 0AA House of Lords Information Service, House of Lords, London SW1A 0PW
Phone/email	Commons Information: 020 7219 4272 hcinfo@parliament.uk Lords Information: 020 7219 3107 hlinfo@parliament.uk Summer opening: 0870 906 3773
Hours	In session hours vary. Generally the House of Commons Public Gallery is open Monday and Tuesday from 2:30 p.m. to 10:30 p.m., Wednesday 11:30 a.m. to 7:30 p.m., Thursday 10:30 a.m. to 6:30 p.m., and Fridays (when in session) 9:30 a.m. to 3:00 p.m. Hours for the House of Lords also vary but are similar. Summer opening hours vary. During July and August, hours are usually Monday, Tuesday, Friday, and Saturday from 9:15 a.m. to 4:30 p.m.; Wednesday and Thursday from 1:15 p.m. to 4:30 p.m. There is often a September-October opening with slightly different hours.

Parliament—Palace of Westminster

Time Required	Depends upon how long you have to wait in line. Summer opening tours last 75 minutes.
Admission	When Parliament is in session admission is free. Summer opening tickets are reasonably priced. There are discounts for children and seniors. Children under age four get in free. Tickets are available at the ticket office located on Abingdon Green, across Abingdon Street from Parliament, or online at the Parliament website.
Facilities	Baby-changing area. No coat check, but strollers must be left at security checkpoint. Most areas are wheelchair accessible.
Website	www.parliament.uk

Where? When? £?

Parliament Past and Present Exhibit

Location	Jewel Tower, just across the street from Parliament buildings
Tube	Westminster station (Circle and District lines)
Address	Jewel Tower, Old Palace Yard, Abington Street, London SW1 P 3JY
Phone	020 7222 2219
Hours	Daily from 10:00 a.m. to 5:00 p.m. Closes at 4:00 p.m. in November through March. Last admission is one hour before closing. Closed December 24-26 and January 1.
Time Required	15-30 minutes
Admission	Tickets are inexpensive. There are discounts for children.
Facilities	None
Website	www.english-heritage.org.uk

Where? When? £?

Benjamin Franklin House

Location	On Craven Street, just east of Trafalgar Square
Tube	Charing Cross station (Bakerloo and Northern lines)
Address	36 Craven Street, London WC2N 5NF
Phone	020 7930 6601
Hours	Wednesday through Sunday from 10:00 a.m. to 5:00 p.m. Evening openings on Fridays. Also open Mondays during June through September.
Time Required	45 minutes
Admission	Tickets are reasonably priced. There are discounts for children and students. Tickets can be booked online and must be picked up at the New Players Theatre box office at The Arches shopping passage, just a few feet down Craven Street.
Facilities	None. Not wheelchair accessible.
Website	www.benjaminfranklinhouse.org

Covent Garden—By George I Think She's Got It!

Video buffs can rent *My Fair Lady* and see Covent Garden as it was a hundred years ago (at least according to composers Lerner and Lowe). The market figures prominently in the musical whose central character, Eliza Doolittle, was a Covent Garden flower girl. But Covent Garden's history, like most of London's, is much older. In medieval times, monks from Westminster Abbey grew and sold vegetables in this area and the name Covent Garden is supposedly a corruption of *convent* garden—a reference to the abbey.

There were fruit, vegetable and flower markets at Covent Garden from the medieval era up to 1974. The markets moved out and were replaced by the modern incarnation of Covent Garden—an entertaining variety of shops, cafés, and restaurants. The Covent Garden area houses an eclectic collection of stores, pubs, theaters, and a museum or two.

In a return to its origins, Covent Garden holds an elaborate flower festival every June. The festival features landscapes, flower displays, and demonstration gardens along with entertainment and performances at nearby churches and other venues.

On any summer afternoon or evening you're likely to find a variety of street performers or *buskers*, in the piazza near the old market. The only cost is your conscience, so drop some pence into the hat if you appreciate the entertainment. Over several trips, our kids gawked at fire eaters, a man who danced and spun on his head (wearing a helmet), and a thick-skinned individual who lay down on a bed of nails and invited an audience member to walk on his stomach. Does the admonition "Don't try this at home" sound familiar?

Inside the Covent Garden central market building, which looks vaguely like an old train station, you'll find other more costly entertainment:

- Venture into an old-fashioned toy store
- Browse through a bookstore
- Visit the ice cream parlor (children rarely object to this stop)
- Grab a bite to eat at one of several cafés and restaurants

The merchants operating in Covent Garden have become a bit less unique in recent years as competition from corporate giants like The Body Shop and Gap have muscled aside some independent retailers. Despite this trend, Covent Garden retains enough of its retailing quirkiness to distinguish itself from the average mall or festival marketplace.

In good weather, some of Covent Garden's cafés serve meals *al fresco*. The food varies in type, quality, and cost, but this is generally a good place to get kid-friendly fare. Covent Garden has a number of full-fledged restaurants such as Orso, an upscale Italian place with another location in New York.

Covent Garden is more than just the old marketplace. The streets around this area, especially northwest towards Seven Dials, are a warren of shops, bars and restaurants. For a high cholesterol treat, stop by Neals Yard Dairy, one of the most extensive cheese shops in the city.

After dark, especially on weekends, the crowds around Covent Garden are full of young bar-hoppers. Some of this spills out onto the streets and can be a little disconcerting when walking through the area with young children, but Covent Garden's crowds are generally unthreatening. On summer weekends the area is so overrun with tourists and revelers that Transport for London sometimes restricts access to the Covent Garden

Tube station. Not to worry—it is an easy walk to Leicester Square, or even to Trafalgar Square, where you can catch the Tube or a bus.

Transport Museum

Right next to Covent Garden's central market is a museum that attracts children like a magnet. Where else in London can you get behind the controls of a subway train and take a virtual journey through the tunnels of London's Tube?

At the Transport Museum kids and interested adults can climb on old trams and buses, "drive" several vintages of Tube trains, and buy popular Transport for London souvenirs. The museum employs costumed actors who interact with (and occasionally startle) young visitors.

The Transport Museum has large-scale KidZones where younger children can push buttons, spins signs, and generally touch and play with everything. The museum features a drop-in activity room where kids can grab some crayons and color transportation-related pictures. The museum's shop is the place to purchase popular Transport for London merchandise. All told, if your kids love buses, streetcars, and subways, the Transport Museum is worth a visit.

A complete renovation in 2007 took what was already one of the most popular sights in Covent Garden and transformed it into an even more family friendly attraction. There are new galleries, *driver's eye* simulators, and extra room to display more of the Transport Museum's collection.

Theatre Museum

Covent Garden's Theatre Museum closed in 2007. Dramatic arts have not abandoned the area because the Royal Opera House is a huge presence just behind Covent Garden Market. Most performances here are targeted at an adult audience, but the Royal Opera does offer occasional programs for children. Check the Opera's website at www.royaloperahouse.org.

*　　　　　　*　　　　　　*

Where? When? £?

Covent Garden—Transport Museum

Location	At the east (Russell Street) end of the piazza which surrounds Covent Garden market
Tube	Covent Garden station (Piccadilly Line)
Address	39 Wellington Street, Covent Garden, London WC2E 7BB
Phone/email	General information: 020 7379 6344 Recorded information: 020 7565 7299 enquiry@ltmuseum.co.uk
Hours	The museum is open every day except Friday from 10:00 a.m. to 6:00 p.m. daily. Friday hours are 11:00 a.m. to 6:00 p.m. Last admission at 5:15 p.m. Closed December 24-26.
Time Required	45 to 90 minutes
Admission	Tickets are reasonably priced and children under age 16 get in free. There are discounts for students and seniors.
Facilities	Toilets, baby-changing areas. Most areas are wheelchair accessible.
Website	www.ltmuseum.co.uk

War And Peace

The grand old Duke of York,
He had ten thousand men;
He marched them up to the top of the hill
And he marched them down again!

—Traditional children's song

Cabinet War Rooms and Churchill Museum

Bombs away! If your kids are interested in World War II, or even if they're not, the Cabinet War Rooms may prove fascinating to them. The war rooms were the underground headquarters used by Winston Churchill during the blitz attacks on London.

Most kids enjoy exploring hidden areas so walking through the warren of underground conference rooms, passageways, sleeping quarters, communications centers, and map rooms is a big hit. For a little education along with your exploration, use the audio headphones provided free with each admission. The commentary isn't boring and listening to it slows down kids who tend to fast-forward through historical displays. There is even a special audio tour for kids and the War Rooms' website has a downloadable trail map for children.

There is no guarantee that kids will love the Cabinet War Rooms, but this sight is more interesting than your average museum and children may actually learn something about 20th century history. Chances are that many kids have learned a bit about World War II in school, from movies, or from a grandparent, but the details are often pretty vague.

There are other World War II-related tourist venues in London. Some, like the Britain At War Experience, are commercial recreations, but the Cabinet War Rooms are authentic. After the war ended, many of the rooms were simply closed off and left untouched for years beneath a government office complex. The Imperial War Museum, which operates the Cabinet War Rooms, has done a careful job of restoring the site to its wartime appearance.

Almost all of the wartime underground complex has been opened to the public. One expansion renovated the Churchill family's private quarters including Mrs. Churchill's bedroom, a private dining room and an underground kitchen. But the most ambitious expansion added the definitive Churchill Museum to the Cabinet War Rooms in 2005.

The museum transports the visitor through Churchill's life, though it's not a strictly chronological review of that life. Instead, it presents five thematic chapters: Young Churchill, War Leader, Cold War Statesman, Maverick Politician and Wilderness Years.

There's more British historical detail here than the average American visitor may want to absorb and the contents of the Churchill Museum could be a bit dry for some children. But the museum makes full use of computer and video technology to enliven that history for the casual visitor, while allowing buffs to delve deeper into the Churchill story. The spine of the museum is Lifeline, a 50-foot-long video table that presents an interactive timeline of Churchill's life. Visitors can explore more than 300 data points, encountering some programmed "Easter egg" surprises that will delight, or at least startle, those gathered around the huge video screen.

The museum even interactively captures a few of Churchill's personality quirks. The man was fond of the carp stocked in the fish pond at his Chartwell family home. Churchill would dangle his hand on the water's surface and the fish would gently nibble his fingers. Sure enough, the museum has a tiny "pond" and electronic fish appear when a visitor touches the Plexiglas surface.

Churchill ranks as one of the most quotable speakers of the 20th century, and the museum resounds with recordings of his famous speeches. It also traces his life with more traditional exhibits, such as an Enigma machine that helped break German wartime communication codes, part of an effort he called "the geese that laid the golden eggs." Other artifacts include Churchill's siren suit, custom-made velvet engineer's coveralls that he preferred as casual wear (the suit looks ridiculous to the modern fashion eye). Uniforms, document reproductions and a model of Churchill's Chartwell home are also on display.

Near the end of the museum stands the famous front door to No. 10 Downing Street, a poignant reminder of the man who twice served as prime minister.

Imperial War Museum

London has an entire museum devoted to war—the Imperial War Museum. The war museum tries not to glamorize war, in fact, there are a few fairly graphic exhibits here that may not be suitable for younger children. At the risk of sounding militaristic, the Imperial War Museum offers a wealth of interesting hardware: guns, tanks, airplanes, and rockets. Although some of the equipment is marked "do not touch" there are also many hands-on exhibits. The war museum presents some mini-seminars for children—we saw four kids sitting in a life raft learning about survival at sea from a costumed guide.

The museum has a re-creation of trench warfare in the First World War and another showing life in a London air raid shelter during the Second World War Blitz. The trench warfare exhibit is too graphic for younger kids, and may be upsetting to older people too, with its realistic depiction of the sights, sounds and smells of life and death in World War I trenches. The simulation of the London Blitz invites visitors to sit in a darkened bomb shelter listening to sirens, explosions, and the frightened conversations of wartime Londoners. The ground shakes (surprise!) and you exit onto a bombed-out London street. This may be enough of the Blitz for most people, making a visit to the separate Britain At War Experience superfluous.

The Imperial War Museum gives American visitors a British perspective on several conflicts. Some American children, if they know anything about World War II, think the war in Europe began with the Normandy invasion. British war efforts started years before D-Day and this history is chronicled at the Imperial War Museum. Dunkirk, the Blitz, and the Battle of Britain become much more real after a visit here.

Britain At War Experience

What was it like to live through World War II in London? While the Imperial War Museum and Cabinet War Rooms both provide insights, the Britain At War Experience focuses on the life of London's civilians during the war.

Visitors enter the exhibit through a simulated Underground lift (elevator) and step into a recreation of London during the war. You walk through a bomb shelter, a wartime club, and a shopping area. But the reality of the war in London hits most in the museum's bombed-out street with the sounds of air raid sirens, the cries of trapped victims, and the smell of burning debris. Obviously, this could be too intense for some young children.

What may be most compelling to modern-day children and parents are the experiences of families separated during the war. The Britain At War Experience tells the story of London's children who were relocated away from their homes to the English countryside during the war. Not only did many of these children face the terror of war, they were torn away from their homes and families.

The Britain At War Experience calls itself *Winston Churchill's* Britain At War Experience, which seems a bit presumptuous. Unlike the Cabinet War Rooms and Churchill Museum, the Britain At War Experience is a commercial venue, not a historical site in its own right. The Britain At War Experience is hardly museum-quality either and there is no comparison between this commercial tourist attraction and the top-notch Imperial War Museum (and the War Museum is free, to boot).

The Florence Nightingale Museum

Lo! in that house of misery,
A lady with a lamp I see,
Pass through the glimmering gloom,
And flit from room to room.

—*Santa Filomena* by Henry Wadsworth Longfellow

The Florence Nightingale Museum portrays another side of warfare—a story of mercy and dedication in the face of misery. Florence Nightingale was the "lady with a lamp," a dedicated British nurse during and after the Crimean War. The museum's major exhibit is a re-creation of a medical ward from that conflict. For children or adults who are interested in nursing or the Florence Nightingale story, the museum is an educational stop, but this is not a major tourist destination.

*   *   *

Where? When? £?

Cabinet War Rooms and Churchill Museum

Location	Underneath the Treasury Building, just off Horse Guards Parade Road across from St. James's Park
Tube	Westminster or St. James's Park stations (Circle and District lines)
Address	Clive Steps, King Charles Street, London SW1A 2AQ
Phone/email	020 7930 6961 cwr@iwm.org.uk
Hours	Daily from 9:30 a.m. to 6:00 p.m. Last admission 5:00 p.m. Closed December 24-26.
Time Required	One to two hours
Admission	Tickets are moderately priced and children under age 16 get in free. There are discounts for students and seniors.
Facilities	Toilets and baby changing areas onsite. Café (no outside food allowed). Most areas of the museum are wheelchair accessible.
Website	www.iwm.org.uk

Where? When? £?

Imperial War Museum

Location	South Bank of the Thames, southeast of Parliament
Tube	Lambeth North station (Bakerloo line) or Elephant and Castle station (Northern line)
Address	Lambeth Road, London SE1 6HZ
Phone/email	020 7416 5320
	mail@iwm.org.uk
Hours	10:00 a.m. to 6:00 p.m. daily. Closed December 24-26.
Time Required	Two hours
Admission	Free
Facilities	Toilets and baby changing areas onsite. Café with children's menus, outside picnic area. Most areas of the museum are wheelchair accessible.
Website	www.iwm.org.uk

Where? When? £?

Britain At War Experience

Location	South Bank between Tower Bridge and London Bridge
Tube	London Bridge station (Northern line) or Tower Hill station (Circle and District lines) and across the river
Address	64-66 Tooley Street, London Bridge SE1 2TF
Phone/email	020 7403 2171
Hours	Open daily from 10:00 a.m. to 6:00 p.m. Closes at 5:00 p.m. in October through March. Last admission one hour before closing. Closed December 24-26.
Time Required	One hour
Admission	Tickets are moderately priced. There are discounts for families, children, students, and seniors. Children under age five get in free.
Facilities	Toilets on site. No food. Most areas are wheelchair accessible.
Web Site	www.britainatwar.co.uk

Where? When? £?

Florence Nightingale Museum

Location	South Bank, right across the river from Parliament, on the site of St. Thomas' Hospital
Tube	Waterloo station (Northern or Bakerloo lines), or use Westminster station (Circle and District lines) and walk over Westminster bridge
Address	2 Lambeth Palace Road, London SE1 7EW
Phone/email	020 7620 0374 info@florence-nightingale.co.uk
Hours	Monday through Friday from 10:00 a.m. to 5:00 p.m. Open on weekends and Monday holidays from 10:00 a.m. to 4:30 p.m. Last admission is one hour before closing. Closed Good Friday, Easter Saturday, Easter Sunday, and December 24 through January 2.
Time Required	One hour
Admission:	Tickets are reasonably priced. There are discounts for families, children, students, and seniors.
Facilities	Toilets onsite. Most areas of museum are wheelchair accessible.
Website	www.florence-nightingale.co.uk

Museums—Some Serious, Some Not

He gazed and gazed and gazed and gazed,
Amazed, amazed, amazed, amazed.

—Rhyme for a Child Viewing a Naked Venus in a Painting
by Robert Browning

When we planned our first London trip, our family decided to avoid spending valuable vacation time on things we could do at home. That ruled out meals at McDonald's, Pizza Hut, and the Hard Rock Cafe. There are lots of department stores at home too, so we gave them only a passing visit in London. Finally, since our kids had toured a fair number of museums at home, we decided to visit only a few museums in London.

Realistically, most kids have limited patience to devote to art exhibits and museums. In this realistic vein, when you plan to visit museums in London, consider limiting the time you spend in the museums and the number of things you try to see in each. Be prepared to miss a lot because kids often fast-forward through museums, leaving placard-reading parents in their wake. Satisfy yourself with seeing the highlights and getting the flavor of each museum. Hopefully, you can return to London and see more when the kids are older or tour London's museums without the children on an adult trip in the future.

On the other end of the spectrum, we were taken aback with the cultural choices some tourists make when contemplating a trip to Britain.

Parents planning a youth soccer league trip asked us what the team should see if they had only one free day in London. It took us only a second to respond "No question, go to the Tower of London." They did consider the Tower, but other team parents were lobbying for a bowling and video game amusement center in central London. So the parents group put the itinerary up for a vote. The result? The kids went to the amusement center on their one day in downtown London. Based on that experience, we have decided not to include information about video arcades or amusement centers in this book. We have nothing against them *per se*, and we suspect that anyone who really wants to have this game experience in London will find it.

London has dozens of serious museums, but the term "serious" does not preclude family fun. We'll review several important and unique museums:

- The world-renowned British Museum located in north central London.
- A cluster of three very different museums—Natural History, Science, and Victoria and Albert—in South Kensington.
- The introspective Museum of London near London's financial district.
- And on a lighter note, we'll walk through a museum devoted to toys and one devoted to a world-famous fictional detective.

British Museum

When I first came up to London I had rooms in Montague Street, just around the corner from the British Museum, and there I waited, filling in my too abundant leisure time by studying all those branches of science which might make me more efficient.

—from *The Memoirs of Sherlock Holmes*
by Sir Arthur Conan Doyle

The British Museum is the most famous museum in England—perhaps in the world—and it has a lot to offer from a kid's perspective. Even the briefest walk past one or two of the museum's highlights elicits reactions from children:

- The Rosetta stone—"I can't believe they let you touch it!"
- A mummified cat—"Yuck, gross" (followed by) "Here kitty, kitty."

The British Museum is so huge that it can overwhelm visiting families and quickly go from thrilling to tiring. The only survival strategy is to focus on a few museum highlights, pick a theme, or look for things that appeal to your children's special interests. Read up on the British Museum before you go—nothing looks quite as pathetic as tourists with young children standing in the lobby, studying a map, and trying to decide which way to head in this huge museum. The kids start getting antsy, the parents become frazzled, and the visit is off to a bad start. One solution is to take the family audio tour or follow one of the museum's family trails.

The British Museum was founded in 1753, making even the museum a "museum piece." Despite its age, the British Museum continues to evolve. They've got long-standing permanent displays from Egypt, Western Asia, Greece and Rome; Prehistoric and Roman era British items; and extensive Medieval, Renaissance, Modern and Oriental collections. At one time the British Library shared space here, but it moved to separate quarters in 1997. With the added space, the British Museum made major changes in its Great Hall exhibition area. By enclosing a center courtyard, the museum was able to add an education center. The Ford Centre for Young Visitors primarily serves visiting school groups, but on weekends and holidays this area is used for special family events and activities.

The British Museum's website includes an extensive special section for children. Browsing the site is one way to peak kids' interest before a visit. The website also lists upcoming special family events and activities. Keep an eye out for occasional family-oriented museum tours.

While most museums have strict hands-off policies concerning their exhibits, the British Museum features one area called *Hands On*. Located in the central Reading Room, and other areas of the museum, Hands On is your chance to touch and examine a select, and presumably sturdy, sample of ancient artifacts.

Natural History Museum

There are natural history museums of stature in many major cities and London is no exception. So there is nothing uniquely British about the concept of this museum, but the London version is superb.

With subject matter including volcanoes, dinosaurs, and ecology, natural history is a natural magnet for children. But like many museums, London's Natural History Museum must compete for the attention of children and adults who are used to seeing elaborate computer graphics and animation. The Natural History Museum succeeds in getting a "wow" out of visitors who have seen dinosaurs come to life in *Jurassic Park*.

The museum's exhibits include some realistic animated dinosaurs, a simulated womb, and a "creepy crawlies" exhibit suitable for the anthropoid lovers in the family. There is a huge blue whale suspended overhead in one room, and visitors can experience a simulated earthquake elsewhere in the museum. Some mild cautions: the dinosaurs are shown graphically munching on a less fortunate fellow; the subject matter for the human biology exhibit may evoke interesting questions from younger children; and if spiders make you uncomfortable, the creepy crawlies display is not for you. The whale is tame, and the earthquake is fun.

The museum's Darwin Centre houses 22 million specimens—sometimes referred to as "gross stuff in jars"—collected on the voyages of Captain James Cook, Charles Darwin and countless other scientists. On a behind-the-scenes tour, kids can get a close-up look at this pickled menagerie.

Like the British Museum, the Natural History Museum tries to offer a good number of special events for children and families, including tours, workshops, and even puppet shows. Children under age seven can borrow an explorer backpack, complete with pith helmet and binoculars. Check the museum's website for the latest offerings.

Victoria And Albert Museum

From a child's perspective, this museum dedicated to the decorative arts presents a stark contrast to its neighbors, the ever-popular Science and Natural History museums. Go ahead, ask your children if they want to tour a large museum featuring exhibits on the history of fashion, textiles, ceramics, and jewelry. We suspect the answer will be obvious, especially when that museum is so close to all the cool stuff in the Science and Natural History museums.

Despite this, the Victoria and Albert Museum staff deserves credit because they at least *try* to interest children. Young visitors can borrow an activity backpack at the museum's front desk. The backpacks relate to different areas of the museum and contain tactile activities (discovering objects by feel while blindfolded), quizzes (a museum treasure hunt) and other fun things for kids to do. Nothing is going to turn the V&A into a children's museum, but the backpacks make a family visit survivable. Visitors can also pick up a copy of the *Family Trails* guide from the museum's information desk. The guide outlines a treasure trail that kids can follow through the museum. An activity cart for children is available on Sundays and some school holidays, and there are a number of hands-on exhibits scattered throughout the museum.

Science Museum

Visit the Science Museum on a trip to London and you may have a problem: once your children get inside this museum, they may refuse to leave! The focus of the Science Museum is high tech, hands-on, interactive and up-to-date, with just a smidge of history.

The displays reach out and grab a child's attention like no other museum in the city. Start with the Launchpad, which looks like a giant indoor playground. Kids playing here may not realize that the Launchpad is really a huge physics lab. There are exhibits on fluid dynamics, suspension construction, weight, force, and other physical properties. Kids don't just look at the exhibits or press a few buttons, they climb on machines and make them work. There's an undercurrent of cooperative play here, since several of the experiments will only function if visiting children join together in a group effort. A model rocket spins around overhead, but it only works if four kids synchronize four air pumps. Another conveyer belt/lift contraption moves beans from one end to the other with the cooperation of five or six operators. There are dozens of stations in the Launch Pad so it can accommodate a large crowd of kids and they can all get their hands on something.

The Launchpad is appropriate for children ages six and older (and their parents!), but the museum has not forgotten younger kids. The basement Garden is an interactive area where three- to six-year-olds can experiment through play. For ages seven to eleven a similar area—simply called "Things"—is right next door. Pattern Pod is another favorite gallery for kids under age eight. Older children will enjoy producing a show in the radio and recording studio located upstairs in the museum. There's an admission charge for the museum's Virtual Voyages exhibit—a 20-minute motion simulator ride that adds a bit of amusement park excitement to the Science Museum.

The Science Museum devotes one complete area to an exhibit on materials. In the middle of this area, suspended from the ceiling, is the complete framework of a house. The museum has constructed familiar objects out of unusual materials. A glass bridge transverses the gallery and on quiet days you can hear it "sing" harmonically as you walk across.

The Science Museum is a popular destination for school groups and it can get a little crowded at times. If you are visiting while British schools are in session, plan to arrive either early or late in the day. The museum is well-designed to accommodate crowds and it even offers indoor areas where school groups can eat brown bag lunches without overrunning the museum's café. The café is an acceptable place for a snack or light lunch and it serves special box lunches for kids.

With all it has to offer, the Science Museum does not rest on its laurels. The museum has an elaborate new wing and is constantly updating its displays. So when you finally drag your kids out of the museum, you can promise a return visit on a future trip to see what's new at the Science Museum.

Museum Of London

London is chock-full of museums dedicated to various forms of art and history. The Museum of London takes an introspective view—the subject is London itself. The museum examines London from prehistory to present-day. This modern museum provides visitors a history lesson, showing glimpses of old London from Roman artifacts to recreated 18th century prison cells. One of the museum's prize displays is the Lord Mayor's coach. The coach is elaborate, but if you have already visited the Royal Mews, you've probably seen enough ceremonial coaches for one visit.

The Museum of London is a good rainy day venue for older children and adults, with well-designed displays that use an interactive time-line to trace the history of London. Kids peer with morbid fascination at the small diorama depicting the great London fire, and the artifacts from the abandoned Roman city of Londinium are also interesting. The

Museum of London is built right along the old Roman city wall, a portion of which forms one side of the museum's inner courtyard.

A great deal of London's history revolved around its place at the center of Britain's seagoing empire. The Museum of London operates the Museum in Docklands, housed in a restored 200-year-old Georgian warehouse at Canary Wharf. The museum contains countless artifacts that tell the story of the Docklands, warehouses, and trade. The museum's Sailortown gallery is a full scale recreation of the dark and dubious local streetscape frequented by sailors in the mid-1800s. But the Mudlark gallery may be most fascinating to kids. *Mudlarks* are people who search the muddy banks of the Thames looking for treasure, usually finding junk, but occasionally unearthing valuable artifacts. The Mudlark gallery contains a play area for younger kids and interactive exhibits for older children.

Victoria Museum And Albert Museum Of Childhood

This branch of the Victoria and Albert Museum claims to be one of the largest toy collections in the world and it certainly has an impressive array of dolls, doll houses, stuffed animals, games, trains, puppets, and costumes. The Museum of Childhood leans toward the static display of toy antiquity rather than the hands-on, interactive exhibits that many children have come to expect. But the museum is not completely static and a renovation in 2006 did much to update the displays. Children under five will enjoy the indoor soft play area and another spot where they can dress up, play with giant dominoes and explore a huge doll house. There's also a roving "art trolley" for the crafty and a board game playing area.

Because of its location in east London, the Museum of Childhood is fairly out of the way for most tourists, but this is a popular venue for school groups. London once had two more museums devoted exclusively to children's playthings. Unfortunately, the London Toy and Model Museum's real estate was worth more than its value as a tourist attraction and the museum closed. Pollock's, a toy shop and museum, met a similar fate.

Sherlock Holmes Museum

Are we *sure* that Sherlock Holmes was a fictional character? Using our powers of deductive reasoning, we've determined that Mr. Holmes is indeed a fake. So this museum is a fake too—an elaborate, fun, and almost believable fake filled with Sherlock Holmes memorabilia. In the famous detective's study, kids can put on a deerstalker hat, pick up a meerschaum pipe and utter the inevitable "Elementary, my dear Watson" to their hearts' content.

The museum is operated by the Sherlock Holmes Society. Kids visiting the museum receive small souvenirs, such as a postcard, detective's badge, or Mr. Holmes' business card.

Tourists visiting other places in London are sometimes approached by costumed characters who distribute Sherlock Holmes calling cards advertising the museum. Don't be put off by the advertising, this museum near Regent's Park is worth a stop. Holmes' fans can also visit a 9-foot-high statue of the detective standing outside of the Baker Street Underground station.

*   *   *

Where? When? £?

British Museum

Location	Bloomsbury, north of New Oxford Street
Tube	Tottenham Court Road station (Central, Northern lines), Russell Square station (Piccadilly line), or Holborn station (Central, Piccadilly lines)
Address	Great Russell Street, London WC1 3DG
Phone/email	020 7323 8299
	information@thebritishmuseum.ac.uk
Hours	Museum galleries are open Saturday through Wednesday from 10:00 a.m. to 5:30 p.m., Thursday and Friday 10:00 a.m. to 8:30 p.m. Some individual exhibits have shorter hours. The Great Court is open Sunday through Wednesday 9:00 a.m. to 6:00 p.m., Thursday through Saturday 9:00 a.m. to 11:00 p.m. The Reading Room viewing area is open until 8:30 p.m. on Thursdays and Fridays. Closed December 24-26, January 1, and Good Friday.
Time Required	How much time have you got and how patient are your children? You can skim the highlights in two hours or spend days here.
Admission	Free except for some special exhibits
Facilities	Restaurant and cafés (no outside food allowed). Baby-changing areas, nursing area. Coat checks. Most areas of museum are wheelchair accessible.
Website	www.thebritishmuseum.ac.uk

Where? When? £?

Natural History Museum

Location	In Kensington, just south of Hyde Park
Tube	South Kensington station (Piccadilly, Circle, and District lines)
Address	Cromwell Road, London SW7 5BD
Phone/email	020 7942 5000 information@nhm.ac.uk
Hours	Open daily from 10:00 a.m. to 5:50 p.m. Last admission at 5:30 p.m. Closed December 24-26.
Time Required	Several hours
Admission	Free except for some special exhibits
Facilities	Restaurant, cafés and snack bar. Indoor and outdoor picnic areas. Baby-changing areas. Coat check. Most areas of museum are wheelchair accessible.
Website	www.nhm.ac.uk

Where? When? £?

Victoria and Albert Museum

Location	In Kensington, just south of Hyde Park near the Natural History Museum
Tube	South Kensington station (Piccadilly, Circle, and District lines)
Address	Cromwell Road, London SW7 2RL
Phone/email	020 7942 2000 vanda@vam.ac.uk
Hours	Daily from 10:00 a.m. to 5:45 p.m. Also open every Wednesday and the last Friday of each month until 10:00 p.m. Closed December 24-26.
Time Required	An hour or less with kids in tow; longer if patience allows.
Admission	Free
Facilities	Café and restaurant. Indoor and outdoor picnic spots. Baby-changing/nursing room. Coat and package check. Most areas of museum are wheelchair accessible.
Website	www.vam.ac.uk

Where? When? £?

Science Museum

Location	Just south of Hyde Park, near the Victoria and Albert Museum
Tube	South Kensington station (Piccadilly, Circle, and District lines)
Address	Exhibition Road, South Kensington, London SW7 2DD
Phone	0870 870 4868
Hours	10:00 a.m. to 6:00 p.m. daily. Closed December 24-26.
Time Required	Several hours
Admission	Free. Special exhibits and the IMAX Cinema cost extra. Family passes are available.
Facilities	Several restaurants, indoor picnic area. Baby-changing areas. Unattended coat check. Most areas of the museum are wheelchair accessible.
Website	www.sciencemuseum.org.uk

Where? When? £?

Museum of London

Location	A couple of blocks north of St. Paul's Cathedral
Tube	Barbican station (Circle and Metropolitan lines)
Address	London Wall, London EC2Y 5HN
Phone/email	0870 444 3851 info@museumoflondon.org.uk
Hours	Monday through Saturday from 10:00 a.m. to 5:50 p.m., Sunday noon to 5:50 p.m. Last admission at 5:30 p.m.
Time Required	One to two hours
Admission	Free
Facilities	Café, picnic areas. Toilets and baby-changing areas. Coat check. Museum is wheelchair accessible.
Website	www.museumoflondon.org.uk

Where? When? £?

Museum in Docklands

Location	Docklands, east of the Tower of London
Tube	West India Quay (Docklands Light Railway) or Canary Warf (Jubilee line)
Address	West India Quay, Canary Wharf, London E14 4AL
Phone/email	0870 444 3851 info@museumoflondon.org.uk
Hours	Open daily from 10:00 a.m. to 6:00 p.m. Last admission at 5:30 p.m. Closed December 24-26 and January 1.
Time Required	One to two hours
Admission	Tickets are reasonably priced. Children under age 16 get in free.
Facilities	Café, restaurant. Toilets and baby-changing areas. Museum is wheelchair accessible.
Website	www.museumindocklands.org.uk

Where? When? £?

Museum of Childhood

Location	In east London, at the corner of Cambridge Heath Road and Old Ford Road
Tube	Bethnal Green station (Central line)
Address	Cambridge Heath Road, London E2 9PA
Phone/email	020 8983 5200
Hours	Daily from 10:00 a.m. to 5:45 p.m. Last admission is at 5:30 p.m. Closed December 24-26 and January 1.
Time Required	One hour (longer if you attend an activity or workshop)
Admission	Free
Facilities	Cafés (no outside food allowed), outdoor picnic area. Baby-changing areas. Coat and package check. Museum is wheelchair accessible.
WebSite	www.vam.ac.uk/moc

Where? When? £?

Sherlock Holmes Museum

Location	Near the southwest corner of Regent's Park
Tube	Baker Street station (Bakerloo, Jubilee, Metropolitan, and Circle lines)
Address	221b Baker Street, London NW1 6XE
Phone/email	020 7935 8866
	info@sherlock-holmes.co.uk
Hours	9:30 a.m. to 6:00 p.m. daily. Closed December 25.
Time Required	30 to 45 minutes
Admission	Tickets are reasonably priced. There are discounts for children. Tickets can be booked online.
Facilities	Most areas of museum are not wheelchair accessible.
Website	www.sherlock-holmes.co.uk

Fun, But Undeniably Tacky

Madame Tussaud's Wax Museum
—Gee, Don't They Look Lifelike?

First, a disclosure: not everyone in our family is a fan of wax museums. There's something undeniably weird about these worlds of wax and we tend to avoid the macabre, which seems to be a staple of the wax museum industry. Remember, Madame Tussaud began her career by displaying the death masks of people executed during the French Revolution. Fortunately, visitors to Madame Tussaud's have an option to skip scary parts. If you want to bypass the dripping, disgusting chamber of horrors and stay with entertainers, sports figures and famous folks, just follow the signs.

Wax figures are lifelike, but they lack certain human qualities like mortality and ego, so the museum can come up with some combinations that would be improbable in real life. There's nothing to prevent a wax Michael Jackson from communing with a wax Gandhi, or the Pope from kibitzing with Madonna. To our knowledge, the museum has yet to display those unlikely combinations, but Madame Tussaud's can allow King Henry VIII to gather all his wives together in one room without anyone losing her head. Elvis is here, too (guess he wasn't abducted by space aliens after all). Visiting American children will recognize many of the figures in the Wax Museum, but not all, especially the British football players.

Wax Museum visitors can climb into the shell of a London taxi and take a brief ride highlighting the history of the city. In a couple of minutes, you are whisked past the great fire, the building of St. Paul's, the Victorian era, the Blitz, and back to present day London. Good news—no taxi driver, so no tip is required.

Our biases about wax museums are certainly not shared by everyone because Madame Tussaud's is one of the most visited attractions in London. Lines to get into the museum are often long, but they move fairly fast. Since it is over 200 years old, Madame Tussaud's almost qualifies as a historic sight itself, albeit a very commercial one. But consider for a moment: what does a wax figure of Elvis have to do with a visit to London?

Scaring Children—Definitely Not Fun And Way Beyond Tacky

Parents traveling with young children should be aware of this phenomenon: some exhibits, especially wax museums, dungeons, and the like, are designed to frighten the daylights out of most kids and many adults. Madame Tussaud's is an offender and the London Dungeon is *definitely* one of the worst. To give you an idea of just how perverse the London Dungeon is, here's a description taken from a visitor's guide:

> *Exhibition depicting the darker side of British Medieval History, Death, Torture, Damnation and Disease. The dark, slimy vaults contain Trials by Ordeal, History of Capital Punishment and the Tortures used in the Tower of London ... .A major attraction is The Jack the Ripper Experience—a 20 min multi-media exhibition throughout the year. Also on display are the 'headcrushers' from France and the Spanish 'garrotters'.*

Need we say more? To see *real* dungeons, head for the Tower of London.

And while they're not designed to scare, a number of London exhibits and commercial museums employ live costumed actors who liven up their boring jobs by standing mannequin-still, then suddenly springing to life. Be aware of this practice and at least make sure the kids visit the restroom ahead of time.

*   *   *

Where? When? £?

Madame Tussaud's Wax Museum

Location	South of Regent's Park, just down the street from the Sherlock Holmes Museum
Tube	Baker Street station (Circle, Bakerloo, Jubilee, or Metropolitan line)
Address	Marylebone Road, London NW1 5LR
Phone/email	0870 999 0046 csc@madame-tussauds.com
Hours	9:30 a.m. to 5:30 p.m. on weekdays and 9:00 a.m. to 6:00 p.m. on weekends. Closed December 25.
Time Required	Two hours
Admission	Tickets are expensive. There are discounts for children, seniors, and families. Late afternoon admission is less expensive, as are tickets that don't include the *Chamber* horror show. Timed tickets are available for an extra fee. Tickets can be booked online.
Facilities	Coffee shop onsite. Toilets available. Bag and stroller storage areas available. Most areas are wheelchair accessible.
Website	www.madame-tussauds.com

Where? When? £?

London Dungeon

Location	On the south bank of the Thames near London Bridge rail station.
Tube	London Bridge station (Northern and Jubilee lines)
Address	28/34 Tooley Street, London SE1 2SZ.
Phone	020 7403 7221
Hours	Daily from 10:00 a.m. to 5:00 p.m. Hours vary by season and during holiday periods. Closed December 25.
Time Required	One hour (less if you run out screaming right away)
Admission	Tickets are expensive. There are discounts for children, and seniors. Tickets are available online.
Facilities	Most areas are wheelchair accessible.
Website	www.thedungeons.com

On The River

HMS Belfast

While standing on Tower Bridge, it is impossible to miss the huge warship anchored just upstream in the Thames. The HMS Belfast is a retired World War II cruiser, now open to the public and operated as a floating museum. Visiting the Belfast is not really all that different from visiting any one of several retired U.S. warships on display in coastal American cities, but if you're a warship aficionado, and you're in the neighborhood, stop by the Belfast. Many kids love exploring the maze of decks, passageways, and compartments in this old warship.

Golden Hinde—Famous Ship, Strange Name

This is another of the growing number of tourist stops sprinkled along the south bank of the Thames—a full-scale reconstruction of the 16th century ship that Sir Francis Drake sailed around the world. The ship is moored at St. Mary Overie Dock, just up the river from London Bridge. Like the original, the new Golden Hinde sailed around the world, but the new ship started its journey in California in 1973.

History buffs visit the ship because Sir Francis Drake's accomplishments personify the height of British sea power; children may want to stop here just to see the boat. Those who want to get more in touch with the salty life of tall-ship sailing can even arrange to spend the night onboard in one of the Golden Hinde's occasional living history events. Berths are on the hard wooden lower decks, so bring a pillow!

If you are in the area, consider walking just a bit further to Southwark Cathedral. Although little known to tourists, this is one of the finest medieval churches in London. Local resident John Harvard was baptized in the cathedral in 1607. He went on to found Harvard University. Other Southwark residents leaned more toward infamy than fame. The nearby exhibition on the site of the old Clink Prison is *not* a recommended family sight given its vivid recreation of the brothels that graced this former red-light district.

*   *   *

Where? When? £?

HMS Belfast

Location	Floating along the south bank of the Thames, just upstream from Tower Bridge. Enter from a pier on the South Bank or take a shuttle boat from Tower Pier at the Tower of London. Shuttle runs every 15 to 30 minutes between 11:00 a.m. and 5:00 p.m.
Tube	South bank: London Bridge station (Northern line) North bank: Tower Hill station (Circle and District lines) and cross the river on Tower Bridge
Address	Morgan's Lane, Tooley Street, London SE1 2JH
Phone/email	020 7940 6300
Hours	Open daily March through October from 10:00 a.m. to 6:00 p.m. Closes at 5:00 p.m. in November through February. Last admission is 45 minutes before closing. Closed December 24-26.
Time Required	One to two hours
Admission	Tickets are reasonably priced. Discounts for students, and seniors. Children under age 16 get in free.
Facilities	Café onsite. Some areas are not wheelchair accessible. Toilets available.
Website	www.iwm.org.uk

Where? When? £?

Golden Hinde

Location	On the south bank of the Thames, just upstream from London Bridge
Tube	London Bridge (Jubilee and Northern lines) or Monument station (Circle and District lines) then walk across London Bridge
Address	St. Mary Overie Dock, Cathedral Street, London, SE1 9DE
Phone/email	0870 011 8700 info@ goldenhinde.co.uk
Hours	Open daily from 10:00 a.m. to 6:00 p.m. Call to confirm opening times.
Time Required	30 minutes to an hour. Longer for special events.
Admission	Tickets are reasonably priced. There are discounts for children, families, and seniors.
Website	www.goldenhinde.org

PART 2

Hey Kids! Let's . . . .

Go To The Park

I want always to be a little boy and to have fun. So I ran away to Kensington Gardens and lived a long long time among the fairies.

—from *Peter Pan* by J. M. Barrie

London has some of the most beautiful urban parks in the world. Stroll through them as a family and everyone is happy—adults can admire English gardening miracles while children just run and play. Never underestimate the value of simply sitting on a park bench and soaking up the atmosphere of London (unless it is raining—that's not the "atmosphere" you'll want to soak up). In warm weather, lawn chairs are spread across London's expansive parks. A word of caution: if you sit down, you've rented a chair. To relax for free, sit on a park bench or a picnic cloth.

While parents may plan a sophisticated, expensive overseas trip, sometimes their children would just as soon stay home and go to a playground (or worse, watch TV). Since you are reading this book, you may have already chosen to ignore this truth. You are sure that a visit to London will be an educational, horizon-broadening experience for the whole family. Absolutely correct, but don't rule out letting your kids hit the playgrounds and parks as part of your trip.

For the visitor with younger children, playgrounds serve two purposes. First, they are a good break from an intense schedule of sightseeing. Forced to behave themselves in hotels, restaurants, cathedrals, theaters, and museums, most kids can stand to burn off some energy on a playground. The second purpose of playgrounds is simple bribery. You just might be able to get through that last museum gallery if you bribe your kids with the promise of a playground break. Fortunately, you don't have to look far for a playground in London because they're located in big parks and shoehorned into tiny lots between buildings.

St. James's Park And The Green Park

St. James's Park tops our list as the most beautiful park in central London. Situated between Buckingham Palace and the government offices at Whitehall, St. James's is an island of green surrounded by many of London's prime historic sites. The park you see today was designed by John Nash in 1827, but it has been a royal park since King Henry VIII acquired St. James's in the early 16th century.

There aren't many playgrounds here, and even walking on the grass is not allowed in some areas, but St. James's Park is still a great place to take children. Before your trip, rent the movie *101 Dalmatians* (the live-action version starring Glen Close, not the animated film). St. James's Park is the site of the frantic bicycle chase scene that ends when Pongo and Perdita's human masters land in the park's lake. In this same lake, kids can spot pelicans, flamingos, and rare black swans—some of the 20 species of waterfowl that live in the park. Look for the shy black swans at the island nearest Whitehall, hiding beneath overhanging tree branches. All the birds gather round when the pelicans are fed by the park staff at about 3:00 p.m. during the summer months.

The Green Park is just across the street from St. James's Park and, until recently, was known as Upper St. James's Park. Here "recently" refers to the mid-1700s since The Green Park dates back to the 1500s. Once used as a dueling ground, The Green Park is now just another pleasant spot with tall trees and broad lawns serving as a buffer between the palace and Mayfair's busy Piccadilly thoroughfare.

The flowery grounds of St. James's Park are beautiful to look at, while The Green Park is a prime spot to rent a lawn chair and relax. The parks are not all nature and quiet gardens though. St. James's hosts band concerts twice daily in the summertime. And the peace and quiet is truly shattered when artillery gun salutes are fired from one of the parks.

Hyde Park And Kensington Gardens

Hyde Park, along with the adjoining Kensington Gardens, forms a massive expanse of green in the core of London. Hyde Park dates back to the early 1500s when it was a royal hunting ground. The park packs a wealth of activities kids will enjoy:

- Boating on the serpentine lake (canoeing, rowing, paddle boats)
- Seasonal swimming from the Lido
- Fishing in the Serpentine Lake
- Lawn bowling and putting greens
- Tennis
- Playgrounds
- Band concerts (on Sundays and bank holidays from May through August)

We've noted that St. James's Park was a playground for Dalmatians Pongo and Perdita. Well, nearby Kensington Gardens has its own story for children: Peter Pan lived here. He's still here—let your kids find the Peter Pan sculpture in Kensington Gardens. Don't get too excited, it is just a statue, but if you *believe*....

The search for Peter Pan's pirates draws long lines of London children to Kensington Gardens where a popular playground evokes the memory of two of Kensington's most famous residents: the unlikely pair of Princess Diana and Peter Pan. Opened in 2000, the Diana,

Princess of Wales Memorial Playground features a pirate ship, a water play area and teepees, along with conventional swings and slides.

Nearby Kensington Palace was Diana's official home and the star-crossed princess often sought anonymous refuge in Kensington Gardens. The Diana Memorial Playground is on the site of an earlier playground donated by *Peter Pan* author J. M. Barrie.

But it's the playground, not the memorial or literary connections that attracts kids like no other place in Kensington Gardens. The two acre site is dominated by a fully-rigged pirate ship seemingly grounded on a beach. Children can climb a hidden passage between the galleon's three decks and even try to re-float the ship by moving sand out of the ballast. The park's beach cove (watch out for the crocodiles!) is a water play area where kids can search for the imprints of fossils and even a mermaid's tail.

When visiting children tire of the pirate ship and cove, they can move on to the treehouse camp and call each other using the park's "tree-phones." Then it's on to the Native American teepees, or maybe a stop in the Movement and Musical Garden to make music, or at least joyful noise. The Peter Pan theme continues into the park's restroom facilities, located in the "Home Under The Ground." Don't remember your Peter Pan? This was where the Lost Boys lived.

Kensington Gardens are essentially a western extension of Hyde Park. Together, they form a green oasis stretching from the backyard of Buckingham Palace all the way to Kensington Palace. Other highlights here are the gardens around Kensington Palace, a model boat sailing pond, a seasonal restaurant, areas for kite flying, and a puppet theater.

The Diana Memorial Fountain is located just south of the Serpentine Bridge in Hyde Park. The memorial to the late princess is one of the most-visited areas of any park in London. The flowing waters of the Diana Memorial are low-key, as royal monuments go, in contrast to the nearby ornate Albert Memorial erected by Queen Victoria to honor her beloved husband Prince Albert.

During summer months, Hyde Park often hosts rock concerts and other huge events. It pays to check the events listing for the park if you want to attend an event or to avoid the crowds.

Go Horseback Riding

Young equestrians and their parents can gain a different perspective on Hyde Park by signing up for a group ride at Hyde Park stables. Five miles of trails wind through the park, allowing visitors to combine horseback riding with sightseeing. Riders can trot along the famous Rotten Row bridle path and canter beside the park's Serpentine lake.

Hyde Park stables offer group rides and children are welcome. No previous riding experience is required. There is a weight limit of 175 pounds for horseback riding. The stables provide riding helmets and boots.

The Regent's Park

The largest park in downtown London is located on the northern border of the city center. The Regent's Park, like many others, began its life as royal hunting grounds during the reign of Henry VIII and the park was landscaped by John Nash in the early 1800s.

There's a little of everything here. Regent's Park is sports-oriented with a running track, athletic fields, and—although it doesn't quite seem cricket—American softball. During the warm months, the scent of roses wafts from Queen Mary's Garden in the center of the park. A stroll north lands you at London Zoo. In summer, Regent's Park hosts an open air theater featuring Shakespeare's *Midsummer Night's Dream* and other popular productions. There is even a children's boating lake where kids can captain small paddle boats in a specially constructed shallow pond. And yes, Regent's Park has playgrounds (three of them).

Visit The Park After Dark?

In England, there was scarcely an amount of order and protection to justify much national boasting. Daring burglaries by armed men, and highway robberies, took place in the capital itself every night ...

—from *A Tale of Two Cities* by Charles Dickens

Based upon Charles Dickens' description, London street crime was a real problem in 1775. While today's street-wise travelers generally avoid city parks after dark, London's central parks still *feel* relatively safe, even at night. Crime exists in London, but violent street crime is not common. The most threatening sights we've seen during evening walks in St. James's and Green Parks were the guards on patrol around the a royal residence—we rounded a corner and faced two camouflaged soldiers carrying automatic weapons! Although many parks officially close in the evenings, their pathways are still used by late night urban strollers. Normal precautions apply.

★   ★   ★

Where? When? £?

St. James's Park and The Green Park

Location	St. James's Park is between Buckingham Palace and Horse Guards Parade. The Green Park is just north of St. James's Park, closest to Buckingham Palace
Tube	St. James's Park station (Circle and District lines)
	Green Park station (Jubilee, Victoria, and Piccadilly lines)
Address	The St James's Park Office, The Store Yard, St. James's Park, Horse Guards Parade, London SW1A 2BJ
Phone	020 7930 1793
	stjames@royalparks.gsi.gov.uk
Hours	St. James's Park is open from 5:00 a.m. to midnight. The Green Park is open 24 hours.
Time Required	You can speed through in 30 minutes, stroll for an hour, or spend an afternoon relaxing here.
Admission	Free
Facilities	Toilets in The Green Park are at the northeast corner near the Green Park Tube station. In St. James's Park, toilets are at the east end near HorseGuards Parade and in the center at Marlborough Gate. Cafés and restaurant, plenty of picnic opportunities.
Website	www.royalparks.gov.uk

Where? When? £?

Hyde Park and Kensington Gardens

Location	West of Mayfair and north of Kensington, stretching from the end of Buckingham Palace Gardens all the way to Kensington Palace
Tube	The area is ringed by Tube stops. For Kensington Palace use High Street Kensington station (Circle and District lines) on the south or Queensway station (Central line) on the north. Other stations along the north border of the park are Lancaster Gate and Marble Arch (both on the Central line). Stations along the south are Hyde Park Corner and Knightsbridge (both on the Piccadilly line).
Address	Park Manager, Rangers Lodge, Hyde Park, London W2 2UH
	Kensington Gardens Office, Magazine Store Yard, Magazine Gate, Kensington Gardens, London W2 2UH
Phone/email	020 7298 2100
	hyde@royalparks.gsi.gov.uk kensington@royalparks.gsi.gov.uk
Hours	Most areas are open from 5:00 a.m. until midnight, but the gardens around the Palace are open from 6:00 a.m. to dusk. The Diana Memorial Fountain opens at 10:00 a.m. and closes based upon daylight hours.

Hyde Park and Kensington Gardens

Time Required	This is almost two miles long so seeing all of it will take a while. Spend an hour or an afternoon.
Admission	Free
Facilities	Toilets in several locations. Cafés, restaurants, snack bars, and plenty of picnic spots. Most areas of the parks are wheelchair accessible.
Website	www.royalparks.gov.uk

Where? When? £?

Diana Memorial Playground

Location   In the northwest corner of Kensington Gardens, near Kensington Palace

Tube   Queensway (Central line)

Phone   020 7298 2141

Hours   The playground is open to children age 12 and under. Unaccompanied adults may tour the playground from 9:30 a.m. to 10:00 a.m. only. The playground opens at 10:00 a.m. and closes based upon daylight hours. Last admission is 15 minutes before closing. Closed December 25.

Time Required   Who's asking? Kids may not want to leave at all.

Cost   Free

Facilities   Café. Toilets and baby-changing areas.

Website   www.royalparks.gov.uk

Where? When? £?

Hyde Park Stables

Location	Just north of Hyde Park, near the Long Water lake
Tube	Lancaster Gate station (Central line)
Address	Hyde Park Stables, 63 Bathurst Mews, London W2 2SB
Phone/email	020 7723 2813 info@hydeparkstables.com
Hours	Weekdays from 7:15 a.m. to 5:00 p.m. On weekends, the stables open at 9:00 a.m.
Time Required	An hour or longer, plus time to saddle up
Cost	Hourly rates are very expensive
Website	www.hydeparkstables.com

Where? When? £?

Regent's Park

Location	North of Marylebone area and less than a mile northwest of Hyde Park
Tube	Baker Street station (Circle, Bakerloo, Jubilee, or Metropolitan line), or Regent's Park station (Bakerloo line)
Address	Park Manager, The Store Yard, Inner Circle, Regent's Park, London NW1 4NR
Phone	020 7486 7905
Hours	5:00 a.m. to dusk
Time Required	Whatever you wish
Admission	Free
Facilities	Toilets in several locations. Cafés, restaurants, snack bars, and plenty of picnic spots. Most areas of the parks are wheelchair accessible.
Website	www.royalparks.gov.uk

Go Cruisin'

'Believe me, my young friend, there is nothing—absolutely nothing—half so much worth doing as simply messing about in boats.'

—from *The Wind in the Willows* by Ernest H. Shepard

This section is devoted to cruising in London. Since this is a family travel publication, we define cruising in a family-friendly way: riverboat cruises on the Thames, a unique amphibious tour on the river *and* through town, canal boat cruises on Regent's Canal, and a cruise (actually more of a "spin") on the London Eye.

River Cruises

Taking a boat ride in London can serve many purposes:

- The water view gives a unique perspective of many of London's famous sights.
- Sometimes, a boat is the most practical way to get where you're going.
- The phrase "Hey kids, let's go on a boat trip!" is usually received with more enthusiasm than "Hey kids, let's go into this cathedral."

Boating on the Thames is a practical and fun way to reach several destinations from central London: down river to Greenwich, Canary Wharf and the Thames River flood barrier; upriver to Richmond, Kew, and Hampton Court; a quick shuttle trip from the Tower of London to the HMS Belfast floating museum; or just a sightseeing cruise between

Tower Bridge and Westminster. Transport for London—the Tube and bus company—operates or coordinates most river services. There has been a concerted effort to expand the use of the Thames by commuters as well as pleasure cruisers and the Transport for London website lists a dizzying array of river boat routes.

Before you take a cruise to someplace like Hampton Court, decide how much time you want to spend on a boat because Hampton is a four hour boat ride from London. The Thames loops and turns, so river trips can take much longer than other modes of transportation. On a more manageable scale, visitors can take 50-minute evening sightseeing cruises from several London river piers. If the weather is nice, this makes a relaxing, low-key evening activity. And sunset on the Thames can be magnificent!

Hop Aboard The Duck

Can't decide whether to take a bus tour of London or a boat tour on the Thames? You can do both onboard a "DUKW." These craft started out as World War II amphibious vehicles, capable of waddling through rivers and driving overland. Refitted and painted bright yellow, these strange looking hybrids take visitors on a 70-minute land and water tour from near the London Eye, through central London, before splashing-down into the Thames and returning to the London Eye.

Yes, the bright yellow DUKWS look out of place (some would say tacky) rumbling past Big Ben. That won't faze most children. The Duck Tour is a big hit with many visiting families.

Canal Boats

There's no better way to get to London Zoo than to cruise on a narrow boat up or down Regent's Canal. Of course, you don't have to stop and see the animals; canal cruises are just a great way to relax and see some off-the-beaten-path parts of London. Walking the canal towpath is also possible and there are some interesting Regency buildings, iron bridges, and tunnels along the way. London's canals connected the city's manufacturing centers before railways took over, so there are also some run-down, formerly industrial areas along the canal.

Camden Town, at one end of the Regent's Canal boat trip, is not always an ideal place to explore with younger kids. The weekend crowd-crush can be daunting for a family trying to walk together. Camden Town on a summer weekend is like wandering into a third world marketplace. This is a trendy area where London's young shop for funky fashions, accessories, and handcuffs. The weekend market is hugely popular. Little Venice, at the other end of the canal, is a more sedate locale for tourists getting on or off the canal boats.

The two main canal trips for tourists are a waterbus service between Camden Lock and the London Zoo and a longer sightseeing cruise between Little Venice and Camden Lock. There are other trips available on different portions of Regent's Canal and other London canals.

The London Eye

It's hard to miss this giant Ferris wheel just across the river from Big Ben and Parliament. The London Eye's operators insist that their commercial venture is an *observation wheel*, not a Ferris wheel, but that is a distinction most visitors miss.

Terminology aside, the London Eye is a fantastic vantage point from which to view downtown London. Visitors ride in large observation pods that slowly rotate around the 450 foot-tall wheel. The combination of the slow motion and the enclosed pods makes for a tame ride. Visibility ranges up to 25 miles, so on a clear day you can't see forever, but you might see as far as the town of Windsor. Riding the London Eye at sunset on a clear-to-partly cloudy day is an unforgettable London experience.

* * *

Where? When? £?

Thames River Cruises

Location	London has a number of river piers, but many popular cruises leave from Westminster Pier (just downstream from Big Ben), Tower Pier (near the Tower of London), and Embankment Pier
Tube	Westminster Pier: Westminster station (Circle and District lines)
	Embankment: Charing Cross station (Bakerloo and Northern lines)
	Tower Pier: Tower Hill station (Circle and District lines)
Time Required	The sightseeing boat from Westminster Pier to Tower Pier takes about 20 minutes; a boat from London to Greenwich takes about an hour; Hampton Court is almost four hours up the river from London.
Fares	Fares range widely. The least expensive are short jaunts on commuter boat runs. Some discounts are available if you have a Transport for London Travelcard.
Facilities	Most boats are wheelchair accessible. Larger boats have food concessions, toilets and other facilities.
Website	www.tfl.gov.uk (click on River Services). The site also links to individual commercial boat operators.

Where? When? £?

Duck Tours

Location	Between Waterloo rail station and the London Eye on the south bank of the Thames
Address	London Duck Tours Limited, 55 York Road, London SE1 7NJ
Phone/email	020 7928 3132 enquiries@londonducktours.co.uk
Hours	10:00 a.m. to dusk. Closed December 24-26, 31 and January 1.
Time Required	75 minutes
Admission	Tickets are expensive. There are discounts for children, families, students, and seniors. Tickets can be booked online, with an additional fee.
Facilities	No onboard facilities. Not fully accessible for individuals in wheelchairs.
Website	www.londonducktours.co.uk

Where? When? £?

Regent's Canal Boat Trips

Location	This portion of Regent's Canal runs from Little Venice (just north of Paddington rail station), around the top of Regent's Park, to Camden Lock (east of the park).
Tube	Little Venice: Warwick Avenue station (Bakerloo Line) Camden Lock: Camden Town station (Northern line)
Phone	Jason's Trips: 020 7286 3248 London Waterbus Company: 020 7482 2660
Hours	Waterbus runs hourly from 10:00 a.m. to 5:00 p.m. from April through October. There is limited service in other months.
Time Required	About 90 minutes round trip from Little Venice to Camden Lock
Admission	Tickets are inexpensive. There are discounts for children, seniors, and families. Combination zoo and boat tickets are available.
Facilities	Limited accessibility for individuals in wheelchairs. Toilets at docking points only.
Website	www.jasons.co.uk www.londonwaterbus.com

Where? When? £?

The London Eye

Location	On the south bank of the Thames, just downstream from Parliament and next-door to County Hall
Tube	Waterloo station (Northern or Bakerloo lines), or Embankment station (Bakerloo, Circle, District and Northern lines)
Address	Jubilee Gardens, South Bank, London SE1
Phone/email	0870 990 8883 customer.services@ba-londoneye.com
Hours	10:00 a.m. to 9:00 p.m. from June through September; 10:00 a.m. to 8:00 p.m. from October through May. Closed December 25 and for one week each January.
Time Required	30 minutes for the ride, plus waiting time
Admission	Tickets are moderately priced. There are discounts for children and seniors. Kids under age five ride for free.
Facilities	Fully accessible for individuals in wheelchairs. Toilets, baby-changing facilities, package check. Snack bar available onsite.
Website	www.londoneye.com

Do A Brass Rubbing

Brass rubbings are a fun pastime for kids if the weather turns bad during your visit to London (and it *may*). For the uninitiated, brass rubbings were once actual rubbings of the ancient burial vault brasses of knights and nobility, done on paper using chalk or charcoal. Eventually, all that rubbing began to threaten the survival of the brasses, so copies were cast. Brass rubbing centers have large selections of brass casts and kids can choose to copy knights, ladies, dragons, or other medieval brasses.

Here's the drill. Start by taping a large piece of rubbing paper to the face of the brass plate, then carefully rub across the paper with a special colored rubbing crayon. It's a little like putting a piece of paper on top of a penny and rubbing it with a pencil. After endless rubbing with the crayon, you have a two dimensional copy of the brass. The rubbing center staff will roll up your completed work and place it in a cardboard mailing tube. When you get home, take your brass rubbing to be framed. The best thing about this souvenir is that you made it yourself!

Brass rubbing is a good activity for artistically inclined children from about age seven and up. It takes a while to satisfactorily complete a brass rubbing, so plan at least 30 minutes to an hour or more, depending upon your skill, persistence, and the size of the brass on which you are working.

There are two brass rubbing centers in central London: one at St. Martin-in-the-Fields Church just off Trafalgar Square and one at All Hallows-By-The-Tower Church, near the Tower of London. St. Martin's brass rubbing center is a full-time facility, but All Hallows is only open at very limited times.

Brass rubbings are popular and companies tour elementary schools in the United States to introduce children to this art form. Even if your children have done brass rubbings at home, the variety of brasses doesn't compare with what you find in the London centers, and the atmosphere at someplace like St. Martin's crypt is so much more authentic.

St. Martin's has a cafeteria where hungry brass rubbers can get a quick meal. The cafeteria floor is made of stone slabs that mark the burial places of former church members. It's not as macabre as it sounds. After repeated exposure to England's innumerable abbeys, cathedrals, and churches, children become accustomed to walking over the not-so-recently departed. The St. Martin's cafeteria is fast, convenient, and provides a lot of choices.

While you are here, go upstairs and take a look at the rest of St. Martin-in-the-Fields Church. Many visiting children can't relate to the massive Westminster Abbey as a church, but St. Martin's looks more like a typical American colonial church building. St. Martin-in-the-Fields is home to frequent lunchtime musical recitals. These are relatively brief, informal concerts that most children can sit through with minimal squirming. It's a chance for families to absorb some London culture in a dosage that most children can take. Lunchtime concerts are often given in the church on Mondays, Tuesdays, Wednesdays and Fridays at 1:00 p.m. The concerts are free, but there is a collection at the door.

All Hallows-by-the-Tower Church is, as the name implies, conveniently located near the Tower of London. This is one of the oldest churches in London and certainly worth a quick visit, but All Hallows is hardly a major tourist stop. The brass rubbing center is a volunteer-staffed enterprise, open at limited times, so call or check the church's website before visiting.

        *   *   *

Where? When? £?

St. Martin-in-the-Fields Brass Rubbing Centre

Location	Northeast side of Trafalgar Square. Facing the church, enter down basement steps on the right side of the building (Duncannon Street)
Tube	Charing Cross station (Bakerloo and Northern lines)
Address	The Crypt, St. Martin-in-the-Fields Church, Trafalgar Square, London WC2N 4JJ
Phone/email	020 7930 9306 info@smitf.org
Hours	Monday through Wednesday 10:00 a.m. to 7:00 p.m., Thursday through Saturday 10:00 a.m. to 10:00 p.m., Sunday noon to 7:00 p.m.
Admission	No charge to get in. The cost of brass rubbings depends on their size. You can do a small one for only a couple of pounds.
Facilities	Café onsite (no outside food allowed). Not accessible to individuals in wheelchairs. Toilets and baby changing facilities available.
Website	www.smitf.org

Where? When? £?

All Hallows Brass Rubbing Centre

Location	All Hallows-By-The-Tower Church, near the Tower of London
Tube	Tower Hill station (Circle and District lines)
Address	Byward Street, London, EC3R 5BJ
Phone/email	020 7481 2928 parish@allhallowsbythetower.org.uk
Hours	Limited openings
Admission	Free. The cost of brass rubbings varies.
Website	www.allhallowsbythetower.org.uk

Go Shopping—"Do We Have To?"

> Then, one day, James' mother and father went to London to do some shopping, and there a terrible thing happened. Both of them suddenly got eaten up (in full daylight, mind you, and on a crowded street) by an enormous angry rhinoceros which had escaped from the London Zoo.
>
> —from *James and the Giant Peach* by Roald Dahl

It would be an unlikely surprise to meet the same fate as James' parents while you are shopping in London. It would *not* be a surprise if your children resisted the idea of going shopping as part of your visit. The child's arguments against shopping while on vacation are bolstered by several facts:

- London is an expensive place to shop;
- the Value Added Tax makes things even more expensive; and
- you can find much of the same merchandise back home.

Here's another reason to minimize shopping. You are on vacation in a foreign country, you've spent a lot of money to get here and London offers all kinds of exciting, unique experiences. So why use valuable vacation time doing things you can do at home (like shopping)?

Those biases aside, there is at least one shopping stop which is a guaranteed "must see" for children—**Hamley's Toy Store**. Hamley's was the top commercial highlight of our kids' first and subsequent visits to

London. This is no toy shop; Hamley's is a huge, high quality toy department store on Regent Street. Hamley's has seven floors of toys, and a notable absence of junk. You won't find many bargains here, but you will find some cool toys that are not always available in the United States. Our daughter brought home one art supply item (a hand-held mini airbrush) which was so popular at her school that we had to buy six more for friends and teachers when we went to London the next time. Our advice for shopping in Hamley's: bring your kids and bring your credit cards!

Elegant, curving Regent Street is home to Hamley's and a host of other major stores, including **Liberty**, an upscale emporium located in a mock Tudor building. Many of the stores are unique to London; some you will find at your local mall back home; all are expensive. Oxford Street, at the north end of Regent Street, contains less luxurious shopping, including large department stores **John Lewis, Selfridges,** and **Marks and Spenser.** At times Oxford Street is wall-to-curb with shopping crowds, so grab your child's hands and don't let go.

If your philosophy is "I shop, therefore, I am" you won't be disappointed by **Harrods** in Knightsbridge. But it can be torturous dragging a child through this massive, crowded department store. On the plus side, Harrods has a pet department (kids love it), a toy area (it's no Hamley's), and a stroll through the enormous Harrods food hall is an overwhelming gastronomic event for the whole family.

If you pass by Harrods at night your kids may think the store is decorated for Christmas because the building is outlined by thousands of tiny lights. Unlike many American department stores, Harrods has just two major sales—in July and January—and these events attract crowds of bargain hunters. Also, unlike at your local mall back home, don't try walking into Harrods wearing cut-offs and a T-shirt. The store has a dress code and they enforce it.

By contrast, **Fortnum and Mason** on Piccadilly (street) in Mayfair is shopping on a scale that most people can deal with. The store is impressive and our children remarked that Fortnum and Mason was the only place they've ever bought cookies from someone wearing a tuxedo. The first floor food department is filled with teas, jams, biscuits, and other delicacies at surprisingly reasonable prices for this neighborhood. The quality fashions and other merchandise on Fortnum and Mason's upper floors come with premium price tags, and alas, there's no real toy department.

While in the Mayfair area, take a walk through **Burlington Arcade** and you will discover that the shopping mall is not a new phenomenon. The ornate covered arcade off of Piccadilly was built in 1819 and it is occupied by a series of upscale shops. Mall security guards here look a little different from those at home. With their top hats and formal uniforms, Burlington Arcade's "Beadles" are a combination of security guard and information guide. There's an equally upscale shopping arcade across the street near the Royal Academy of Art.

Another joy of shopping is London's many bookstores, both those selling new and antiquarian books. American readers of all ages will find some different books here than at home. Children can ditch *Goosebumps* for the British *Horrible Histories* series; adults can peruse used book shops for first editions of great English works (although a first edition of a Dickens novel would be a rather expensive souvenir). There are a number of used book stores located just north of Trafalgar Square along Charing Cross Road, between Leicester Square and the Tottenham Court Road Tube station. The booksellers are crowded, dusty shops filled floor-to-ceiling with used, old, and antique books. The economics of running a used bookstore in a city with high rents and high property values threaten the existence of some of London's booksellers. Hopefully, they will be able to survive.

London's street markets and still-functioning traditional food markets offer another look at shopping as it existed before malls and big-box retailing. Depending upon their interests and tolerance for browsing, children may enjoy strolling through street markets and

London's old-style food markets are dramatically different from grocery stores back home. One of the better-known markets consists of antiques and flea market stalls along **Portabello Road**, best visited Saturdays from 8:00 a.m. to 6:00 p.m. (Tube stop: Nottinghill Gate). **Camden Market**, northeast of Regent's Park, is another area filled with flea markets and other quirky goods. Camden has a series of open-air market stalls and storefront shops that generally operate seven days a week (Tube stop: Camden Town). For traditional covered food markets, wait until lunchtime and head to restored **Leadenhall Market**, located in London's financial district (Tube stops: Bank or Monument). Leadenhall is open weekdays from 7:00 a.m. to 4:00 p.m. There's a weekend craft market in **Greenwich** (Docklands Light Railway stop: Cutty Sark). This is just a sampling and there are other markets scattered throughout London, although they tend to be concentrated in areas off the normal tourist track, especially in east London.

Museum shops can sometimes provide unique shopping experiences for visitors. For example, the Transport Museum in Covent Garden is filled with souvenirs sporting popular London Transport graphics and the Museum of London operates a special low-cost shop for children. And while museum shops are not immune to tacky, cheap souvenirs, they also offer books and reproduction items that can't be found elsewhere.

The **Covent Garden** area is filled with specialty shops, especially along Neal Street, just north of the Covent Garden market. Kids will probably enjoy stores here that specialize in kites, skates, cartoon art, and toys. There has been a trend towards fewer independent shops and more big retailing names in Covent Garden, but the corporate giants have not completely taken over. The small streets and alleyways north and west of the Covent Garden piazza and marketplace have a variety of independent shops. Neil's Yard Dairy, for example, is worth a stop to sample from a huge selection of British and European cheeses.

Store hours are a bit more conservative in Britain than in the United States, but things are changing. Department stores are generally open from 10:00 a.m. to 7:00 or 8:00 p.m. with extended hours on Thursdays and/or Fridays. Many stores are also open for limited hours on Sundays, especially department stores and shops in festival-style shopping areas such as Covent Garden or trendy locales like Chelsea. By tradition, some British shops closed daily from 1:00 p.m. to 2:00 p.m., but this has become very rare in big cities like London.

Wherever adults choose to shop in London, they can usually count on free advice from children:

> "The Toy Department," Michael reminded her, "is in *that* direction."
> "I know thank you. Don't point," [Mary Poppins] said, and paid her bill with aggravating slowness.
>
> —from *Mary Poppins* by P. L. Travers

*　　　　*　　　　*

Where? When? £?

Hamley's Toy Store

Location	On the east side of Regent Street, a couple of blocks south of Oxford Street and north of Piccadilly Circus
Tube	Oxford Circus station (Central, Victoria lines)
Address	188—196 Regent Street, London W1B 5BT
Phone/email	0870 333 2455 or 020 7494 2000 hamleys@hamleys.com
Hours	Monday through Friday from 10:00 a.m. to 8:00 p.m., Saturday 9:00 a.m. to 8:00 p.m. and Sunday noon to 6:00 p.m. Seasonal and holiday hours vary.
Time Required	Shop 'till you drop (or go bankrupt)
Facilities	Café onsite. Baby-changing areas, toilets available.
Website	www.hamleys.com

Where? When? £?

Fortnum and Mason Department Store

Location	On the south side of Piccadilly (street) in the heart of Mayfair
Tube	Green Park station (Jubilee, Victoria, or Piccadilly lines)
Address	181 Piccadilly, London W1A 1ER
Phone	020 7734 8040
Hours	Monday through Saturday from 10:00 a.m. to 6:30 p.m. Food hall and one restaurant open Sunday noon to 6:00 p.m.
Facilities	Restaurants onsite. Baby-changing areas, toilets available.
Website	www.fortnumandmason.com

Where? When? £?

Harrods Department Store

Location	Knightsbridge, south of Hyde Park
Tube	Knightsbridge station (Piccadilly line)
Address	87–135 Brompton Road, Knightsbridge SW1X 7XL
Phone	020 7730 1234
Hours	Monday through Saturday from 10:00 a.m. to 8:00 p.m., Sunday noon to 6:00 p.m. Food halls have longer hours.
Facilities	Restaurants onsite. Baby-changing areas, toilets available.
Website	www.harrods.com

Go To The Theater

The theatre was quite full and Paddington waved to the people
down below. Much to Mrs. Brown's embarrassment, several of
them pointed and waved back.

—from *A Bear Called Paddington* by Michael Bond

London's West End theaters offer a vast array of shows, but finding
something appropriate for children can be a challenge. Musicals are
often a good bet if you choose wisely: *Mary Poppins*, not *Chicago; The
Lion King*, not *King Lear*.

One of the best resources for choosing shows is on the internet. The
Society of London Theatre's website at www.officiallondontheatre.co.uk
is, as the name implies, the "official" guide to London theater. The Society
also operates the legitimate half-price ticket booth in Leicester Square.
What's On Stage (www.whatsonstage.com) is a database listing perform-
ing arts events throughout Britain. You can search for events by location,
date, or type of performance. Both websites include theater reviews, seating charts, and even a way to order tickets, albeit with hefty booking fees.
The British branch of Ticketmaster (www.ticketmaster.co.uk) provides a
similar on-line service. After arriving in London, you can pick up copies
of the printed version of *What's On* and other guides like *London This
Week* for information on theaters.

Most of London's major theaters are located in the West End theater
district close to Piccadilly Circus or Leicester Square and there's another
grouping in the Covent Garden area. Since London's museums and
tourist sights usually close by 6:00 p.m., an evening theater performance

works well for many visitors. As a bonus, the theater is a chance to sit down after walking all day. If you don't mind walking a bit more, you can use the Tube to get to most theaters, but a taxi will drop you right at the lobby door. After the show, hailing a taxi can be a challenge since all theaters let out at about the same time and competition for taxis is fierce. The area around Leicester Square, including the Tube stop, is often very crowded with a mixture of theater patrons and a slightly rowdy bar crowd late on Friday and Saturday nights, so extra vigilance is advisable when traveling with children.

How To Get Tickets

There are ticket agencies in the U.S. that sell London theater tickets, but most charge substantial service fees. Armed with information from the internet, you can sometimes order tickets directly from some theater box offices. Yes, it means an international phone call when the London box offices are open (remember the time difference) and once you've charged the tickets, you are locked in. But booking through the box office is often less expensive than using a ticket agent. Keep in mind that many theaters have exclusive marketing deals with commercial ticket agencies and you probably won't be able to bypass this arrangement.

Other possible sources of theater tickets are airlines or travel agencies that sometimes sell theater vouchers to their customers at reasonable prices. The down side is that you generally have to go to a booking agency in London to exchange theater vouchers for available theater tickets. Often you won't know in advance which shows you can see and the voucher exchange process can waste valuable vacation time. However, on our first trip to London we trekked to a ticket agency, exchanged our vouchers, and got fairly good seats to an acceptable play. As compensation for waiting around the ticket office, our children visited their first English playground conveniently located right across the street.

How about half-price theater tickets? While standing in line at a ticket outlet hardly constitutes family fun, it can save money—you'll usually pay half price, plus a fee of two pounds. One drawback is that families traveling together need seats together and these can be hard to find at the bargain outlet. Another problem with the half-price ticket outlet is the limited selection of shows offered since the most popular productions don't need to discount tickets. Be wary of using anyplace other than the official TKKS half-priced ticket offices in Leicester Square and Canary Wharf.

Watch out for ticket touts (scalpers) who ply the Leicester Square area and charge exorbitant rates for sometimes sub-par seats. Scalping of a more organized sort can be found in *bureau de change* (money exchanges) that sell tickets throughout London. Buying tickets, or changing money, at a bureau de change is generally not a good deal.

All these ticket tips aside, one obvious way to get tickets is simply to walk up to the theater box office on the day of the show and see what is available. Theaters occasionally have unsold and returned tickets for even the more popular productions. Finally, if you are desperate to see a popular show, and you are staying in an upscale hotel, check with the concierge. A good concierge can often make rare tickets appear as if by magic—for the right price.

The Globe Theatre

All the world's a stage,
And all the men and women merely players.

—from *As You Like It* by William Shakespeare

Theater thrives in modern London so it is hard to imagine a time in history when playwrights and actors struggled against religious and government suppression. But one reason that the famous Globe Theatre was located on the south bank of the Thames was to escape the unfriendly atmosphere in the City of London. After an unsympathetic landlord raised the land rent, the theater company moved the Globe, piece by piece, from its City location to Southwark.

In 1613, the original Globe Theatre burned to the ground supposedly the result of a cannon shot during a performance of the play *Henry VIII*. A new theater was built on the site, but it only lasted until 1642 when those fun-loving Puritans forced it to close. The Globe was torn down in 1644 and the site was virtually forgotten. It was not until the 1980s that the foundation of the theater was discovered. Unfortunately, the remains of the Globe are buried below a newer (but still historic) building that was constructed on the site.

The Globe you see today is a reconstruction begun under the leadership of the late Sam Wanamaker, an American actor and film director. But to call the Globe a reconstruction is to sell it short. The new Globe was painstakingly completed using authentic Elizabethan building techniques and the result is both a theater and a tourist attraction. If your children won't sit still for a full-fledged Shakespearean production on the Elizabethan stage, at least take the building tour of the legendary theater and a quick look at the adjoining Globe Exhibition.

British Film Institute's London IMAX Cinema

The bfi London IMAX Cinema is next to the roundabout (traffic circle) in front of the Waterloo rail/underground station. Fortunately, there is a pedestrian tunnel entrance so you don't have to dodge traffic to get there. This is one of the largest movie screens in Britain and features IMAX, 3D, and regular movies. Of course the huge screen comes complete with a blow-you-away sound system (earplugs optional?). The British Film Institute also operates educational and performance space at its nearby National Film Theatre.

*　　　　　　*　　　　　　*

Where? When? £?

Half-Price Ticket Booths

Location	In the clock tower building on the south side of Leicester Square and on platforms 4/5 of the Canary Wharf Docklands Light Railway station
Tube	Leicester Square: Leicester Square station (Northern or Piccadilly lines)
	Canary Wharf: Docklands Light Railway
Phone/email	None
Hours	Leicester Square: 10:00 a.m. to 7:00 p.m. Monday through Saturday. Open noon to 3:30 p.m. on Sundays.
	Canary Wharf: 10:00 a.m. to 3:30 p.m. Monday through Saturday.
Other Info	A small fee is added to ticket sales. No choice of seating locations.
Website	www.officiallondontheatre.co.uk

Where? When? £?

The Globe Theatre

Location	On the south bank of the Thames, near the Southwark Bridge
Tube	Mansion House station (Central and District lines) then walk across Millennium Bridge. Alternate is Cannon Street station (Circle and District lines) then walk across Southwark Bridge.
Address	21 New Globe Walk, Bankside, London SE1 9DT
Phone/email	Box office: 020 7401 9919
	Exhibit center: 020 7902 1500
	info@shakespeares-globe.org
Hours	Performances begin at 2:00 p.m. and 7:30 p.m. during the week and at 4:00 p.m. on Sundays. The play season runs from late April through early October. The Exhibition is open from 9:00 a.m. to noon between May and September and from 10:00 a.m. to 5:00 p.m. the rest of the year. Closed December 24-25.
Time Required	Performance times vary. A tour takes about an hour.
Admission	Exhibition and tour tickets are reasonably priced. There are discounts for children, families, and seniors. Costs for performances vary by location from the low-budget *groundlings* (standees in front of the stage) to the more noble gallery seats.

The Globe Theatre

Facilities	Some areas of the theater are not accessible to individuals in wheelchairs. Restaurant, cafés onsite (no outside food). Baby-changing areas, toilets available.
Website	www.shakespeares-globe.org

Where? When? £?

London IMAX Cinema

Location	South Bank, near Waterloo rail/underground station
Address	1 Charlie Chaplin Walk, South Bank, Waterloo, London SE1 8XR
Tube	Waterloo station (Northern line)
Phone	0870 787 2525
Hours	Open daily with shows from 11:00 a.m. to 10:00 p.m. Times may vary.
Time Required	Depends on film length
Admission	Tickets are moderately priced. There are discounts for children and seniors. Tickets can be booked online for a small additional fee.
Facilities	Toilets and baby-changing facilities. Wheelchair accessible.
Website	www.bfi.org.uk

Start Ramblin'

Where am I going? I don't quite know.
Down to the stream where the king-cups grow—
Up on the hill where the pine-trees blow—
Anywhere, anywhere. I don't know.

—*Spring Morning (from When We Were Very Young)*
by A. A. Milne

Britain is a country of walkers, or "ramblers" in Britspeak. Unlike the United States, where private property paranoia keeps strangers from walking through the countryside, British walkers have the right to trek through much of the country. There are over 100,000 miles of public footpaths and rights-of-way in England and Wales—amazing considering the small size of these countries. British hikers refer to themselves as ramblers with good reason, because they truly ramble across the land. Hiking enthusiasts have banded together to form a nonprofit Ramblers Association. The group's website (www.ramblers.org.uk) is a good starting point for anyone interested in walking through the British countryside.

The detailed instructions contained in British walking guides can be fun for children to decipher. Arm them with trail guides that describe walks using phrases like "go over the stile, turn left at the large oak tree, past the stone wall on your left … ." Once kids learn that *stiles* are fence or wall crossings, they are ready for an adventure on the trail.

Wherever you visit in Britain, pick up information on local walking trails. There is no better way to see the country and get beyond the normal tourist routes. For example, while touring the Cotswold's, we were dismayed when we arrived at Bourton-on-the-Water. The tour books had described a pretty, rural town. The reality of Bourton-on-the-Water on a mid-summer day was dozens of tour buses and hordes of visitors. Luckily we were carrying *Short Escapes In Great Britain,* a book detailing off-the-beaten path walks throughout the country. Using that guide we went over stiles, through fields, and around cows, to tiny Wyck Rissington—a village two miles and two centuries removed from Bourton. Wyck Rissington was the quietest village imaginable with no other tourists and no souvenir shops. We ate a Father's Day picnic in an ancient churchyard, then spent a few minutes visiting the village church. A short two-mile hike had taken us from the tourist version of the Cotswolds to the real thing.

But hiking is not limited to rural Britain. A Thames Path winds 180 miles from the river's source in rural Gloucestershire to the Thames Barrier below Greenwich. In the process the path runs through Windsor, Hampton Court and downtown London.

Strictly speaking, you won't find many hiking trails in town, but London is still very much a city for walkers. The Mall—one of the largest and most historic boulevards in London—is closed to vehicles on Sundays so that pedestrians can stroll unimpeded. Before you walk here, make sure your kids know that The Mall in London isn't home to hundreds of stores and a food court. The Mall is the wide street leading from Buckingham Palace along St. James's Park toward Whitehall and the Admiralty Arch. This is one of the most famous parade routes in London and you can make your own parade on any Sunday. The proper pronunciation of Mall rhymes with the word "shall." And just to further the confusion, there are two parallel streets here: The Mall and Pall Mall, a busy street just a few hundred feet north. You can safely stroll down The Mall on Sundays; if you try this on Pall Mall, you'll get run over.

Walking in London does have some hazards, primarily when crossing streets. Tourists from other countries generally look left for oncoming traffic, but because Britons drive on the left, an unwitting tourist may never see the lorry (truck) coming from the right. Smack! One less repeat visitor.

Seriously, the only good defensive strategy is to put your head on a swivel when crossing a street in London. Look right, look left, then look right and left again. That way your instincts won't get you killed. Recognizing the potential hazard, London traffic officials have painted the words "look right" or "look left" on the pavement at some pedestrian crossings.

London crosswalks come in two varieties: painted zebra stripes on the pavement where all traffic *should* stop for pedestrians, and crossings where you must wait for a signal to cross. Zebra stripe crossings are usually further marked by curbside light poles with round, blinking globes to remind drivers to stop for pedestrians.

Assuming you survive crossing the streets, you can take a city walk that traces the outlines of the old wall that surrounded Londinium, the Roman precursor to modern London. This is a 1.5 mile walk between the Museum of London and the Tower of London, with historical markers and glimpses of the old wall along the way.

On the south bank of the Thames, the Queen's Jubilee Walkway runs two miles from Tower Bridge to Lambeth Bridge. There are an increasing number of attractions on the developing South Bank and the area offers spectacular views across the river toward the historic monuments of central London. This is a great walk to take in conjunction with visits to the Globe Theatre, HMS Belfast, Tower Bridge or Tower of London.

For those who want to combine walking with a guided tour, several companies offer walking tours. London Walks is the best known walking tour company, but there are several others. Walks usually focus on an area of the city or a historical theme and are led by guides who are both personable and knowledgeable. Evening walks featuring Jack the Ripper, ghosts, or pub crawls may not be appropriate for children. We found only one downside to signing up for a guided walk—by the time we were ready to start it, we had already walked so much on our own that we were too tired to go.

*   *   *

Where? When? £?

Walking Tours (London Walks)

Location	Walks start outside of Tube stations nearest to the beginning of the walk route.
Address	PO Box 1708 London NW6 4LW
Phone/email	020 7624 3978 Recorded information: 020 7624 9255 London@walks.com
Hours	Starting times from about 10:00 a.m. until mid-afternoon. Evening walks begin at 7:00 or 7:30 p.m.
Time Required	About two hours
Admission	Walks are reasonably priced. There are discounts for seniors and students. Children under age 15 walk for free. Multiple walk discount cards are available.
Website	www.walks.com

Find The Wild Kingdom

You can't be in London for long without going to the Zoo. There
are some people who begin the Zoo at the beginning, called WAY
IN, and walk as quickly as they can past every cage until they get
to the one called WAY OUT, but the nicest people go strait to the
animal they love the most, and stay there....

—from *Winnie-The-Pooh* by A. A. Milne

London's Zoo

London is not a prime travel destination for wildlife seekers. There are
pigeons in Trafalgar Square, exotic waterfowl in St. James's Park, and even
reports of urban-adapted foxes wandering parts of the city. But most
London animals tend to be of the captive variety, so the best spot for
observing animal wildlife in London is probably the zoo in Regent's Park.
Going to a zoo may not meet all your criteria for a "must see" tourist
sight, especially if you've visited other zoos at home. But if you are traveling with children, the London Zoo may still end up on your itinerary.

The London Zoo covers 36 acres in the northern corner of Regent's
Park and is bisected by Regent's Canal. An interesting way to get to and
from the zoo is to take a boat along Regent's Canal (see the *Go Cruisin'*
section). The zoo has operated since 1828 and it fell on hard times in
the recent past, but is undertaking an ambitious expansion program.

The Regent's Park site is one of the oldest zoos in the world, and
sometimes it shows. Nevertheless, the London Zoo has interesting highlights including a gigantic aviary where birds fly "free" and an exhibit

called Moonlight World, designed to fool nocturnal animals into thinking it is nighttime (and letting daytime human visitors see them in action). We dodged the guano and toured the aviary in about three minutes then groped our way through the dark Moonlight World but saw very little animal activity. The zoo's old, dark and leaky aquarium exhibit was also disappointing.

"I want to show you wallaby poop," said the four-year-old to his father. Once the most popular animals in the petting zoo, the shy wallabies suffered from the loving attention of visiting children. The wallabies are gone, replaced by more familiar farm animals that better handle human contact. The children's zoo is a highlight of the London Zoo, not because it includes many exotic species, but because children can interact with the animals displayed here. The petting zoo is conveniently equipped with a hand washing station for use after visiting and touching all the animal friends.

In 1914, at the start of the First World War, an American black bear named Winnie was given to the zoo by a Canadian army officer. Two zoo visitors, writer A. A. Milne and his son Christopher, helped transform the bear into the children's literary classic. Winnie and many other famous residents are history now, and the London Zoo has reinvented itself with a modern theme of "conservation in action." Even with this lofty mission, the zoo knows that visitors still want to see cute, playful animals. When sloth bears were reintroduced to the outdoor exhibits, the bears became the zoo's poster children and when a baby sloth bear was born, the zoo played up the event for all it was worth. The zoo's reptile house even had a small part in *Harry Potter and the Sorcerer's Stone*.

If you live in a place without a zoo nearby, the London Zoo may be a worthwhile stop, even with the relatively high price of admission. If you live near a city with a more modern or less expensive zoo, you may want to bypass the London Zoo.

Something Fishy On The Thames

London boasts a modern aquarium on the south bank of the Thames within walking distance of Big Ben. The Old County Hall, formerly a quasi-city hall for London area governments, has been converted into hotels, shops, and the world class London Aquarium.

With its multi-million liter tanks, the London Aquarium rivals those in Boston, Baltimore, or Long Beach. It is hard to know which theme area children will enjoy most, although the sharks in the Pacific Ocean tank are a good bet, as are the piranhas in the tropical exhibit and the whole rain forest experience. The aquarium is home to 30,000 sea critters, including some that kids can touch. A coral reef exhibit combines the usual aquatic specimens with interactive audio-visual presentations.

County Hall houses an upscale Marriott Hotel, and a moderately priced Travel Inn that is popular with touring family groups. The location is eminently convenient for central London because you can stay here and be within walking distance of Parliament, Westminster Abbey, and the London Eye.

And Something Fowl

Just over three miles west (as the duck flies) from Buckingham Palace, London's wildfowl can make themselves at home in 100 acres of wetlands. The London Wetland Centre opened in 2000 on the site of an abandoned waterworks, creating a wetland habitat that attracts wildlife and human visitors alike. The center staff has counted some 180 wild bird species at the site. The Wetland Centre is not a top tourist destination, but it is popular with local school groups and nature-lovers. The education center and displays are interesting to budding naturalists.

*   *   *

Where? When? £?

London Zoo

Location	On the northern edge of Regent's Park
Tube	Camden Town station (Northern line). Requires a 15-minute walk.
Address	Regent's Park, London NW1 4RY
Phone	020 7722 3333
Hours	Daily from 10:00 a.m. to 5:30 p.m. between March and October. During the rest of the year, the zoo closes at 4:00 or 4:30 p.m. Last admission at 3:00 p.m. Closed December 25.
Time Required	Two hours or so (depends on how much you like zoos)
Admission	Tickets are expensive. There are discounts for families, children, and seniors. Kids under age 3 get in free. Tickets can be booked online.
Facilities	Some areas of the zoo are not accessible to individuals in wheelchairs. Cafés, snack bars onsite. Baby-changing areas, toilets available.
Website	www.londonzoo.com

Where? When? £?

London Aquarium

Location	On the South Bank, just across Westminster Bridge from Big Ben and near the London Eye
Tube	Westminster station (Circle and District lines) then walk across Westminster bridge
Address	County Hall, Westminster Bridge Road, London SE1 7PB
Phone/email	020 7967 8000 info@londonaquarium.co.uk
Hours	Daily from 10:00 a.m. to 6:00 p.m. During peak times, the Aquarium is open until 7:00 p.m. Call or check website to confirm hours. Last admission one hour before closing. Closed December 25.
Time Required	Two hours
Admission	Tickets are moderately priced. There are discounts for children, families, students, and seniors.
Facilities	Fully accessible to individuals in wheelchairs. No food onsite. Baby-changing areas, toilets available.
Website	www.londonaquarium.co.uk

Where? When? £?

London Wetland Centre

Location	Just west of central London, on the south bank of the Thames, about halfway between Buckingham Palace and Kew Botanic Gardens
Tube	Hammersmith station (Piccadilly, District, or Hammersmith & City lines) with a short ride on a connecting "duck bus"
Address	Queen Elizabeth's Walk, Barnes, London SW13 9WT
Phone/email	020 8409 4400 info.london@wwt.org.uk
Hours	In summer months, open daily from 9:30 a.m. to 6:00 p.m. with extended hours on Thursdays. In winter the center closes at 5:00 p.m. Last admission one hour before closing. Closes early on December 24 and closed on December 25.
Time Required	One to two hours
Admission	Tickets are reasonably priced. There are discounts for families, children, and seniors.
Facilities	Accessible to individuals in wheelchairs. Restaurant onsite. Baby-changing areas, toilets available.
Website	www. wwt.org.uk

Watch The Changing
Of The Guard

They're changing the guard at Buckingham Palace—
Christopher Robin went down with Alice.
We saw a guard in a sentry-box.
"One of the sergeants looks after their socks,"
Says Alice.

They're changing the guard at Buckingham Palace—
Christopher Robin went down with Alice.
They've great big parties inside the grounds.
"I wouldn't be King for a hundred pounds."
Says Alice.

—from *When We Were Very Young* by A. A. Milne

What tourist visits London without seeing the changing of the guard? Some do, of course, but we suspect that almost none of them are touring with kids!

Thankfully there are more ways to see changing guards than just crowding against the fence at Buckingham Palace. First, you should know that there are two separate guard ceremonies: the palace guard at Buckingham and the mounted guard down the Mall at Whitehall.

Of the two, the mounted horse guards ceremony is a lot more accessible. The site of the ceremony, a large open plaza called Horse Guards Parade, provides room to spread out and get a good view of the event. At one time the palace of Whitehall stood in this part of London. Horse

Guards Parade was the tiltyard of the palace where jousting tournaments were held.

The guards are mounted troopers of the Household Cavalry, also known as the Sovereign's Life Guard. Hearing this name, children may ask: "If these guys are lifeguards, then where's the swimming pool?" There is no swimming pool, but if your kids love horses, this is *the* guard ceremony to see. The mounted Horse Guards are resplendent with their swords and shining silver breastplate armor and, of course, the beautifully groomed horses. Afterward, your children can even pet the two horses standing guard on the Whitehall Street side of Horse Guards Parade. This makes an excellent kid photo op, but watch where you step!

The horse guards ceremony is a popular event that lasts about 30 minutes. If you just want a glimpse of the horse guards, you can spot them trooping to the ceremony on the park side of Whitehall. The guard leaves the Knightsbridge Barracks in Hyde Park at about 10:30 in the morning and returns around noon.

In mid-June, Horse Guards Parade is the sight of the ceremonial Trooping the Color—a review of troops to mark the Monarch's official birthday. Obtaining tickets to this popular event takes a lot of pre-planning and some luck. It is somewhat easier to attend one of the rehearsals that are held on the weekends preceding the actual event. Massed military bands also gather at Horse Guards Parade on two days in June for the Beating Retreat ceremony. This is a chance to see marching bands and hear the tortured sounds of bagpipes in London.

If you choose to attend the Buckingham Palace guard ceremony be sure to arrive for the changing of the guard early enough to get a standing spot up front against the palace fence so your children have a good view. Even then, be prepared for occasional pushing and jostling for position by other tourists. If it's too crowded for your kids to see, climb up the steps of the nearby Queen Victoria Memorial for a better view. The ceremony is normally performed by the Foot Guards of the British Army's Household Division. In the summer months, the Household

Guard usually wears bright red uniforms with the famous tall bearskin hats (uniforms vary depending upon the season). The changing of the palace guard takes place daily at 11:30 a.m. from April to early August, and every other day during the rest of the year.

Before the ceremony, a military band often plays in the palace court-yard. See if your kids can pick out what they're playing. It's not all old military marches; we once heard a medley of Billy Joel tunes.

You can avoid the crush of the Buckingham Palace guard ceremony entirely by walking down the Mall and turning left on Marlborough Road. After shift change at Buckingham Palace, the relieved guard troop marches away and follows this route to St. James's Palace. Here you can see the retreat ceremony where the guard retires to its barracks. This is not as elaborate as the changing ceremony at Buckingham Palace, but it is a lot less crowded, you are closer to the action, and there's no fence to block your view.

⋆   ⋆   ⋆

Where? When? £?

Changing of the Mounted Horse Guards

Location	Horse Guards Parade, a plaza just off Horse Guards Road near the east end of St. James's Park
Tube	Westminster (Circle and District lines) or Charing Cross (Bakerloo, and Northern lines)
Hours	The horse guard changes at 11:00 a.m. (10:00 on Sundays). Two mounted soldiers stand guard along Whitehall (the street) between 10:00 a.m. and 4:00 p.m.

Where? When? £?

Changing of the Guard at Buckingham Palace

Location	Buckingham Palace
Tube	Green Park station (Jubilee, Victoria, or Piccadilly lines), St. James's Park station (Circle and District lines), or Victoria station (Circle, District, or Victoria lines)
Hours	Daily at 11:30 a.m. during the summer, and every other day during the rest of the year
Time Required	Ceremony lasts 45 minutes, but arrive early to get a decent spot
Website	www.royal.gov.uk

Go Down The River

The Thames will take us to London town,
"Of wonderful beauty and great renown."
The dew goes up and the rain comes down,
To carry us safely to London town.

—*The Thames* by M. M. Hutchinson

Greenwich

Here's a pop quiz for kids who have studied geography: What is the latitude and longitude of London? Give up? At about 52 degrees north latitude London is roughly in line with Calgary, Canada—a lot farther north than you might expect. The second part of the answer is more significant. London's longitude is nearly *zero* degrees since the city sits only a few miles west of the Prime Meridian—the longitudinal line dividing the Earth into eastern and western hemispheres. The suburban London town of Greenwich is the historical home to the Prime Meridian.

Because time is such an important player here, it is hard to visit Greenwich and not keep constantly looking at your watch. Greenwich Mean Time is a standard used by scientists, navigators, militaries, and travelers throughout the world. Once they grasp the significance of Greenwich Mean Time, school-age kids can easily determine the time difference to their hometowns.

Taking the boat down the Thames to Greenwich is pretty neat even if your kids don't give a hoot about longitude and Greenwich Mean Time. (See the *Go Cruisin'* section for more information on boat trips.) But even the most uninterested kids will have a lot of fun on a visit to the Royal Observatory in Greenwich, and they might even learn something.

Interactive exhibits in the observatory teach the importance of longitude to seaborne navigation. Early explorers often sailed in circles because they could measure latitude (distance from the equator) by sighting the angle of the sun on the horizon, but they had no way to accurately measure longitude (distance east or west).

The Royal Observatory was founded in 1675 by King Charles II who appointed John Flamsteed as Astronomer Royal. Flamsteed's marching orders were pretty specific: find a way to measure longitude at sea. Given the competition between England, France and Spain for control of the seas, solving the navigation problem was the Apollo moon project of its day. "Mission Control"—the observatory building—was designed by Sir Christopher Wren.

A detailed explanation of longitudinal navigation is *way* beyond the scope of this book, but the basic premise is that accurate timekeeping is essential to accurate navigation. Thus, timekeeping became a key function of the observatory. Every day at precisely 1:00 p.m. an orange ball slides down a pole on the top of the observatory. In times past, ships on the Thames would set their clocks ("chronometers" to you navigators) by this ball. Like many events in England, there is absolutely no reason to keep dropping the time ball today, but the tradition continues and tourists love it. Greenwich Mean Time remains a world standard for timekeeping, although technically it has been replaced by Coordinated Universal Time.

Continuing with our lecture from *Longitudinal Navigation 101*, another key to navigation is establishing a uniform starting point—the zero or prime meridian line. It wasn't until 1884 that a worldwide agreement set that line in Greenwich. The prime meridian runs right through the Royal Observatory and is marked on the pavement and walls of the building. The meridian officially divides west from east and at Greenwich this dividing line also provides entertainment for visitors.

At the observatory you can stand with one foot in the western hemisphere and one foot in the eastern (or put a foot on the line and balance between east and west).

Greenwich's association with the sea is found in other local sights including the Old Royal Naval College and the National Maritime Museum. Children may enjoy much of the Maritime Museum, especially the All Hands Gallery with its interactive exhibits on diving, gunnery, signals, and other seafaring skills. The Maritime Museum is a good mixture of high tech and history. There are the requisite pictures of old dead navy guys and fleets of ship models, plus more interesting audio-visual and computer simulations.

The Maritime Museum is also home to the Admiral Nelson exhibit, or perhaps we should call it the Nelson shrine. One end of the gallery is dominated by a giant bust of Lord Nelson that scowls over visitors. There is plenty of dry historical material here—items that most kids will skip—but some of the computer animated battle displays will attract young visitors.

While in Greenwich, sailors in the family can tour one of the world's most famous sailing ships. The permanently dry-docked clipper *Cutty Sark* is the last survivor of the ships that sailed around Cape Horn bringing tea from China. Every day at 1:00 p.m. a cannon is fired on the deck of the Cutty Sark, scaring seagulls and tourists alike. Another oddity in Greenwich is the Queens House. Take a close look at this small palace. It seems awfully familiar doesn't it? When you learn that this building was known as The White House, the connection becomes uncanny. The term refers to the building's white plaster facade, but the architecture could have been a model for the White House in Washington, D.C. The Queen's House, Royal Observatory, Old Royal Naval College, and Nautical Museum have been designated as a World Heritage Site by the United Nations.

Greenwich is another stop in the Sir Walter Raleigh trivia tour. A muddy Greenwich street is supposedly where Sir Walter laid his cloak over a puddle to protect the feet of Queen Elizabeth I. The Royal Family returned the favor to Raleigh later (see the *Tower of London* section).

Greenwich was once a peaceful village on the Thames. Given its association with timekeeping and navigation, some influential Britons saw a unique opportunity to focus world Millennium celebrations on Greenwich and they developed an ambitious millennium theme park called the Millennium Dome. Some saw this as progress and the chance to highlight a revitalized, modern Britain. Others saw it as hucksterism of the worst sort. Relatively few tourists saw it at all since the Dome's attendance projections were vastly overestimated. The Millennium Dome was planned as a one year exhibition during 2000, but the structure continues to be used as an entertainment and sports complex.

The Dome is located along the Thames, just down river from old Greenwich. At more than 1,000 feet in diameter and 160 feet high, the Dome is undeniably huge. The Dome and other redevelopment of old docks and industrial land along the Thames profoundly affects the character of historic Greenwich.

Just five miles down the Thames from central London, Greenwich is easy to reach. You can take a boat, the Tube, or the Docklands Light Railway. As you might expect, most children vote for the boat trip (and on a nice day, they're right). Here's a rundown on the easiest ways to get to Greenwich:

- Taking the Tube? The Underground's Jubilee Line goes to the Greenwich North station, the closest stop for the Dome, but not very close to other Greenwich sights.
- Want to try the Docklands Light Railway? This automated above-ground commuter line runs to a station just steps from the Cutty Sark in Greenwich. The Docklands Light Railway connects with the Tube in downtown London.

- The boat? There are frequent trips from downtown London. If you have the time and the weather is good, the boat is a perfect way to see the Thames and get to Greenwich.

Before the Docklands Light Railway Cutty Sark station opened, travelers to Greenwich got off one stop up the line at Island Gardens and then walked through a pedestrian tunnel under the river. The 1,200-foot-long Greenwich Foot Tunnel was built in 1902, and is still operating. Walking under the Thames in the tunnel can be fun, but it is not for the claustrophobic.

For more information on boat trips, read the *Go Crusin'* section. See the *Getting Around Town* section for more on the Tube. It is also possible to reach Greenwich by train from several London rail stations. While the Greenwich rail stop is not particularly close to the town's tourist attractions, there is a shuttle bus service which runs from 10:00 a.m. to 5:00 p.m. during spring and summer.

Thames River Barrier

You can continue down the Thames from Greenwich to visit a modern engineering wonder—the flood barriers that protect London from the ravages of the rising river. If your kids are fascinated by dams, bridges and other big public works projects, then they may enjoy a visit to the Thames River Barrier Information Centre. Once the most futuristic structure on the Thames, the barrier is a minor tourist attraction. Residents upstream in Greenwich would never take the barrier for granted because without it, parts of their town would be underwater during flooding tidal surges.

This is the world's largest moveable flood barrier. When raised, its clamshell floodgates are each five stories high. If you arrive on the day of the scheduled monthly systems test, you don't have to wait for a flood to see the barriers in action. But even when the barriers aren't operating, the visitors center offers informative exhibits and working models. There is a park with a play area and restaurant overlooking the barrier on the north side of the river. There is no direct access between the park and the information centre.

*   *   *

Where? When? £?

National Maritime Museum and Royal Observatory

Location	Greenwich, near the riverfront
Address	National Maritime Museum, Park Row, Greenwich, London SE10 9NF
Phone/email	General information: 020 8858 4422 Recorded information: 020 8312 6565 nmmweb@nmm.ac.uk
Hours	Daily 10:00 a.m. to 5:00 p.m. Open until 6:00 p.m. during the summer months. Last admission is 30 minutes before closing. Closed December 24-26.
Time Required	Two to three hours or more for all three sights (museum, observatory, and Queen's House)
Admission	Free. Special exhibits may have admission fees.
Facilities	Most areas of the museum are accessible to individuals in wheelchairs, but parts of the observatory have limited access. Café and snack bar in museum. Baby-changing areas, toilets available.
Website	www.nmm.ac.uk

Where? When? £?

The Cutty Sark

Location	On the waterfront, near the passenger ferry dock in Greenwich
Address	King William Walk, Greenwich, London SE10 9HT
Phone/email	020 8858 2698 enquiries@cuttysark.org.uk
Hours	Open daily from 10:00 a.m. 5:00 p.m. Last admission is 30 minutes before closing.
Time Required	30 minutes
Admission	Tickets are reasonable. There are discounts for children, families, students, and seniors.
Facilities	Limited access for individuals in wheelchairs
Website	www.cuttysark.org.uk

Where? When? £?

Thames River Barrier

Location	On the river Thames downstream from Greenwich
Transportation	There is rail service from Charing Cross and Waterloo East to Charlton, which leaves you with a 15-minute walk to the barrier. Bus service is also available from east London. The most direct way is to take the boat. The trip is about 75 minutes from central London. The Docklands Light Railway stops at Pontoon Dock for access to the Thames Barrier Park.
Address	Unity Way, Woolwich SE1 5NJ
Phone	020 8305 4188
Hours	The information center is open daily 10:30 a.m. to 4:00 p.m. from April through September and 11:00 a.m. to 3:30 p.m. in other months.
Time Required	One hour
Admission	Tickets are reasonably priced
Website	www.environment-agency.gov.uk www.thamesbarrierpark.org.uk

Go Up The River

Kew—The Smell Of Flowers

Mistress Mary, quite contrary,
How does your garden grow?
With silver bells, and cockle shells,
And marigolds all in a row.

—Traditional children's rhyme

Parks have gardens, palaces have gardens, churches have gardens—you're never far from a garden in London. But if you have not had your fill of gardens during your visit, then add one more sight to your travel itinerary: the Royal Botanic Gardens, better known as Kew Gardens.

Kew Gardens has a more important mission than simply providing an ideal garden for visitors. Plant conservation is the real goal here and Kew's collection contains living specimens of over ten percent of all the world's flowering plants. Another important task at Kew Gardens is the impressive goal to preserve seed samples from *all* the plants on Earth.

But for the casual visitor, the real attractions at Kew are the acres of landscaped gardens and glasshouses full of unusual plant displays. There is enough variety to keep green-thumbed visitors fascinated for days. The rest of us, especially those with children, will probably want to devote two or three hours to simply walking the grounds. A fun fact for bored children: look for the largest flagpole in the United Kingdom, located on the garden grounds.

Kew's elaborate glasshouses are full of surprises. In the basement of the Palm House there is a kid-sized aquarium exhibit. It is not the high tech London aquarium, but the Kew exhibit is just right for a ten-minute visit. The aquarium thoughtfully provides step stools which children can use to get eye-to-eye with the fish.

The world's oldest potted plant is at Kew and anyone who has killed numerous house plants will be amazed that this plant has survived since 1775. Kew also has the world's tallest indoor plant, a replacement for the previous record-holding palm that literally hit the roof in 2001 and had to be cut down. Visiting children may or may not be impressed with all the plants, but kids invariably climb the spiral staircases up to the elevated walkways which encircle the top of the glasshouses. If you lose track of a child, be sure to look up.

Kew's Evolution House is another favorite of children and many adults. These evolutionary plants literally crawl out of primordial ooze that bubbles up near the entrance to the exhibit. The Evolution House is an animated presentation of freshman high school plant biology, cleverly depicting the evolution of plants from the Earth's creation up to modern day. While touring the Evolution House, kids can look for dinosaur tracks and spot eagle-sized dragonflies perched on prehistoric tree trunks. Kew's Climbers and Creepers exhibit is a plant-themed indoor/outdoor playground that mixes learning with play. Kids are free to crawl on and through giant "plants" here.

Although they are nearly eclipsed by the grandeur of the gardens, Kew also contains a small palace and a quaint Royal getaway. Kew Palace was built in 1631 and it is the smallest royal palace in England. Kew was home to King George III who spent time here while suffering from his madness. In 1761 he gave Charlotte, his queen, a nice little wedding present: a rustic cottage built on the Kew grounds and equipped with a menagerie of kangaroos, buffalo, and other exotic animals. The cottage and surrounding grounds remained in the royal family until Queen

Victoria turned them over to Kew Gardens in 1897. Kew Palace was fully restored in 2006 and reopened to the public.

Although there are restaurants on the premises, Kew is a wonderful place to picnic. Its wide-open grounds and fragrant displays are a relaxing contrast to the bustle of other sights in downtown London.

Kew—The Hiss Of Steam

If you have made the trek to Kew, and are not completely exhausted from roaming the gardens, there are some other interesting sights nearby. The Kew Bridge Steam Museum is just across the Kew Bridge from the Royal Botanic Gardens. The museum features several huge working steam pump engines and a small steam railway. On weekends, the museum powers up its huge Cornish steam engines in a great display for kids who like the noise and power of big machines. Kew's steam engines once pumped the water supply for West London and, while the waterworks have been modernized, the giant pumping engines remain on display.

Kew—The Sound Of Music

The Musical Museum falls into a quirky category of tourist attraction. It will never appear on a list of top London area sights, but if you are in the vicinity, and have an appreciation for automatic musical instruments, then plan a brief visit here. You'll be treated to lots of music, but no musicians. Here the instruments play themselves: organs, music boxes, pianos, violins and the Clarabella—sort of a one-man band without the man. Once housed in an old church, the tiny Musical Museum has expanded into larger and modern quarters.

Hampton Court Palace—Oh Henry!

Hampton Court is an extreme example of "keeping up with the Jones's." This elaborate palace was originally built by Cardinal Wolsey in the early 1500s. (The vow of poverty apparently did not apply to the church hierarchy at the time.) King Henry VIII decided that he liked the palace so much that he wanted one just like it. Instead of building his own, Henry borrowed Hampton Court from Wolsey, giving the Cardinal very little choice in the matter.

Much of the intrigue of Henry VIII's reign took place at Hampton Court. Some of Henry's wives enjoyed the palace (briefly) before adjourning to other accommodations in the Tower of London (again, briefly, and in most cases terminally). Henry expanded Cardinal Wolsey's residence and Henry's successors altered the building even more, but portions of Henry's original brick Tudor palace are still visible today. The building changed significantly in the 1600s under King William III who planned to construct an English version of Versailles. William employed Christopher Wren, architect of St. Paul's Cathedral, and converted Hampton Court into one of the finest palaces in Britain.

So how are you going to sell your children on a visit to another palace? Not to worry. In addition to history and architectural splendor, Hampton Court also features Henry VIII's original indoor tennis court, a fantastic garden maze, one of the world's largest grape vines, carriage rides on the grounds, and lots of outdoor space to explore.

We tend to think of Henry the Eighth as Henry the Huge, but in his earlier years he was fairly athletic and a great tennis fan. In 1530 he had a tennis court built at Hampton Court Palace. Royal or "real" tennis is only vaguely like the modern version because this original indoor game was played off the walls and ledges that surround part of the court. Legend has it that Henry played tennis here while Anne Boleyn was executed at the Tower of London. In the modern game, one assumes that most tennis playing kings would stop playing under these circumstances (or at least take a Gatorade break).

The royal tennis court is open to Hampton Court Palace visitors. King Charles II renovated the court in the late 1600s, and what you see today is essentially unchanged since 1700; the obvious exception being the modern-day lighting. Amazingly, the court is still in use and you may be lucky enough to see a game in progress. If so, please observe one basic rule of royal tennis etiquette: spectators must keep quiet!

One of the most popular features of Hampton Court is the famous maze built on the palace grounds for King William III. Children love the challenge of this evergreen maze. Some kids attack the problem logically, tracking their position by the angle of the sun, or by taking only left turns, or using some other semi-scientific approach. Others abandon all logic and just run helter-skelter through the maze. We really don't know which way works best, but the maze is a challenge to adults and children alike. If you buy a ticket to see the palace interior, admission to the maze is included, otherwise there is a small fee to get lost here.

Another interesting stop on the palace grounds is the Great Vine of 1768. The vine is one of the world's largest single grape vines, so immense that it has its own greenhouse and root care field. The old vine is still going, producing a large crop of grapes every year.

The palace gardens alone are worth the trip to Hampton Court. In fact, you can visit some of the grounds for free, so many tourists and local residents simply stroll through the gardens, take a horse-drawn carriage ride, or picnic near the palace. There is also a large tearoom located on the old palace tiltyard. You know times have changed at Hampton Court when you can have tea where Tudor knights once jousted.

While many of Hampton Court's highlights are on the outside, the palace interior is amazing in its own right. Part Versailles, part Tudor brick palace, it is unlike any other palace in Europe. In the restored Tudor kitchens, it looks like the staff is preparing a feast (or maybe just a snack to satisfy Henry VIII's wanton appetite). While children are often interested in the cavernous Tudor kitchens, adults gaze slack-jawed at Henry VIII's opulent Chapel Royal and William III's Baroque state apartments.

Hampton Court is the site of a mammoth flower show held each year during July. Visitors who arrive during the show can expect large crowds, but they will be able to tour a phenomenal gardening exhibition. Admission to the show is separate from the palace and the show tickets are fairly expensive for the casual visitor.

In December and January, a temporary ice skating rink is set up in front of the palace, livening up the site during an otherwise slow tourism period. There are also special events with live actors during the regular season and holiday periods.

   *   *   *

Where? When? £?

Royal Botanic Gardens, Kew

Location	A few miles southwest of central London, along the south bank of the Thames, in the town of Richmond
Tube	Kew Gardens station (District line). Trains from London also arrive at Kew Gardens or Kew Bridge rail stations.
Address	Royal Botanic Gardens, Kew, Richmond, Surrey, TW9 3AB
Phone/email	020 8332 5655 info@kew.org
Hours	The gardens open at 9:30 a.m. daily and close at varying times throughout the year based on daylight. During the summer, last admissions are at 6:00 p.m. on weekdays and 7:00 p.m. on weekends. Buildings may open later and close earlier. Closed December 24-25.
Time Required	Two to three hours or more, perhaps much more if you are a garden lover
Admission	Tickets are moderately priced. Children under age 17 get in free. There are discounts for student and seniors. Separate admission to the palace.
Facilities	Restaurants and snack bars on site. Picnics are allowed in many areas. Toilets and baby changing areas available. Most areas are wheelchair accessible.
Website	www.kew.org

Where? When? £?

Kew Bridge Steam Museum

Location	Just across the river from Kew Gardens, about 100 yards from the north side of Kew Bridge, next to the tall Victorian tower
Tube	The closest Tube stations are Gunnersbury or Kew Gardens (District line), but neither are very close. The Kew Bridge rail station is very convenient and trains run from there to London's Waterloo rail station where you can connect with the Tube.
Address	Green Dragon Lane, Brentford, Middlesex TW8 OEN
Phone/email	020 8568 4757 info@kbsm.org
Hours	Tuesday through Sunday from 11:00 a.m. to 5:00 p.m. Last admission at 4:15 p.m. Steam engines run on weekends and holidays only.
Time Required	One hour
Admission	Tickets are reasonably priced. Children under age 15 get in free. There are discounts for students and seniors. Lower cost tickets on weekdays, when engines are not running.
Facilities	Toilets available. Most areas are wheelchair accessible.
Website	www.kbsm.org

Where? When? £?

The Musical Museum

Location	Across the river from Kew Gardens, just upstream from Kew Bridge
Tube	See Kew Bridge Steam Museum
Address	68 High Street, Brentford, Middlesex TW8 0BD
Phone	020 8560 8108
Hours	Generally open 2:00 p.m. to 5:00 p.m. on weekends during the months of April through October.
Time Required	One hour
Admission	Tickets are reasonably priced. There are discounts for children and families.
Website	www.musicalmuseum.co.uk

Where? When? £?

Hampton Court Palace

Location	East Molesey, Surrey about 10 miles southwest of central London
Transportation	About 30 minutes by train from London's Waterloo station to Hampton Court station, just a short walk from the palace. You can also take the Tube to Richmond and a bus to Hampton Court, but this takes a lot longer. If time is no issue, take a leisurely four hour boat trip up the Thames from Westminster Pier in London.
Address	Hampton Court, East Molesey, Surrey KT8 9AU
Phone	087 0752 7777 (recorded information)
Hours	From March through late October, the Palace is open daily from 10:00 a.m. to 6:00 p.m. The rest of the year, the palace closes at 4:30 p.m. Last admission is one hour before closing. Gardens open from 7:00 a.m. to dusk. Closed December 24-26.
Time Required	Three hours
Admission	Tickets are moderately priced. There are discounts for children, students, seniors, and families. Garden-only tickets are also available. Tickets may be booked online.
Facilities	Self-service restaurant, tearoom. Outdoor picnic spots. Family play/restroom and baby-changing areas. Some rooms of palace are not wheelchair accessible.
Website	www.hrp.org.uk

PART 3

Come On Kids—Field Trip!

London Is Great
—So Why Leave?

London has enough to keep a touring family busy for weeks, so why even consider traveling outside of this fascinating city? Well for one thing, it seems a shame to travel all the way to Britain and not see more of the country than just the capital. The remedy is a field trip—rent a car or take the train and explore some piece of England. By American standards, this is a compact and eminently accessible land. While the focus of this book is London (and nearby places like Greenwich and Hampton Court) we'll give you a hint of what lies further afield by describing a few gems in the surrounding areas:

- Nearby Windsor with its famous castle
- Further afield to Blenheim Palace
- In search of stone circles
- Time out for county churches

We conclude the field trip section with some survival tips for tourists planning to drive in Britain.

Off To Windsor

Although Windsor is within London's suburbs, a family trip here is the perfect opportunity to see a little of the countryside and visit a historic town on the Thames. Windsor Castle, the central focus of the town, is one of the most elaborate castle/palaces in the greater London area. Windsor is an easy 30 to 50 minute train ride from downtown London, so this first field trip requires no driving.

The Castle

Over 900 years ago, William the Conqueror chose the site for Windsor Castle on a hill above the River Thames. Like the Tower of London, Windsor was part of the Norman king's plans to fully subdue and maintain control over England. The strategically placed castle was one day's march to London and served to guard the city's western flank. Subsequent kings and queens used Windsor as a part-time residence and a refuge from wars, plagues and uprisings. What has evolved at Windsor is part Norman castle and part royal palace.

Unlike Hampton Court Palace, Windsor Castle is still used by Britain's Royal family. Since the Castle is a home to Royals and members of their staff, this is another opportunity to let your children look for real-life domestic touches where most visitors just see another historic tourist attraction. On the grounds of the castle you may observe pet cats, resident children walking to school, or staff members off to play tennis. Just like at Buckingham Palace, keep an eye on the flag pole. A Union Jack means nothing special, but if the Royal Standard (the lion flag) appears above the Norman keep at Windsor Castle, the Royals have arrived. During one visit, the Union Jack was flying when we entered the castle and began our tour. After our visit, we hit the rest-rooms and when we came out the Royal Standard was flying. We missed the arrival of the Queen while we were in the loo!

The whole family will enjoy a visit to Windsor Castle. Some of the rooms have extensive displays of armor, which many kids find interest-ing, but of course it can get a little boring going through all those ornate, staid, royal apartments. So a Windsor highlight for most chil-dren is the display of Queen Mary's doll house. This is one of the largest, most elaborate doll houses imaginable, literally fit for a queen. And if they have not had their fill of guards changing already, Windsor Castle boasts a fairly impressive ceremony. Guard changing is every other day at 11:00 a.m., except Sundays, and the schedule alternates monthly between odd or even-numbered days.

One of the most impressive buildings in the castle complex is St. George's Chapel, completed in 1475 and a stellar example of medieval architecture. Eighteen kings and queens are buried here so, yes, Windsor has a full complement of "old dead guys" from a child's perspective. The chapel is often staffed with enthusiastic, knowledgeable volunteer tour guides. On one visit a grandfatherly volunteer took extra time to show off the chapel to our kids, pointing out items of interest to children. This per-sonal touch was an unexpected bonus in a busy tourist attraction like Windsor Castle. Weekend visitors should be aware that the chapel is closed to the public on Sundays and for special events.

Touring Windsor Castle today, visitors see no real evidence of the major fire that destroyed parts of the castle in 1992, but the fire is still a relatively fresh memory here. Young visitors are often interested in the story of the fire and the heroic efforts to save priceless art and furnish-ings from the burning building. About one-fifth of the Castle was dam-aged or destroyed and restoration was completed in 1997 at the cost of almost $60 million. Ironically, the loss at Windsor was actually a gain for London tourists since Buckingham Palace was first opened to visitors in part to help raise money to restore Windsor Castle.

Windsor is a pleasant place to take a walk, a *long* walk. The Long Walk is an arrow-straight road that runs from the east side of Windsor Castle to a statue of King George III nearly three miles away. Closed to most traffic, the roadway is lined by the trees and fields of Windsor Home Park. This is an ideal spot to let children burn off excess energy. They can take off running down the Long Walk, but of course you may have to chase them.

A couple of days each year, visitors to Windsor Home Park can also tour Frogmore House, a royal country estate and burial place of Queen Victoria and Prince Albert. This was a royal house, not a palace, and it is a contrast to the formality of Windsor Castle. The house and gardens are usually open two weekends a year, sometime in May and again in late August.

Windsor—In And Around The Town

The town of Windsor is an amalgamation of history, peaceful English town life along the Thames, and some tacky intrusions by tourist-oriented businesses. It is disconcerting to see a storefront McDonald's and a Pizza Hut just outside the massive ancient walls of Windsor Castle. Sarah Ferguson, the Duchess of York, is reported to have regularly taken her daughters to the Windsor McDonald's (this was probably before she became a spokesperson for Weight Watchers). The tourist traps don't ruin Windsor since they are fairly contained and the rest of the town is generally unaffected.

While in Windsor, take time to walk down to the pedestrian bridge across the Thames to the tiny town of Eton. Eton offers some antique shops, a few pubs, and a glimpse of the famous boys' school whose students have included royal princes. Touring the school—Eton College—is a bit like visiting Harry Potter's Hogwarts Academy. No magic classes and Quiddich matches here, but the buildings and atmosphere of this ancient school seem vaguely familiar to Harry Potter fans. For information about visits, check the school's website at www.etoncollege.com.

More than anything else, Eton is a quiet town on the river; a real contrast to the busy tourist throngs in Windsor. If it is anywhere near teatime as you head back into Windsor, consider stopping at the Orangarie Restaurant located in the Sir Christopher Wren's House Hotel. As the name implies, the hotel was once home to the famous architect. History aside, this is a pleasant place to have tea and watch the swans swimming on the Thames.

All The King's Swans

Walking over the Windsor-Eton pedestrian bridge, it is hard to miss the dozens of swans swimming against the strong current or coasting downstream, always in search of a handout. On one visit, our children counted 60 birds within sight of the bridge.

Since the 12th century, all the swans on the Thames have been owned either by the Royal Family or two other groups: the Vintners and the Dyers. In a land of quaint tradition, it is not surprising that there is a special ceremony for swan herding, or *swan upping*, held on the Thames each July. There is even an official Royal Master of the Swans who supervises the tagging of swans and cygnets. The swan upping on the Thames has become a tourist attraction in itself, but it is difficult for the average tourist to attend because the event moves along the river between the towns of Walton-on-Thames and Whitchurch.

The swans you see at Windsor are so-called mute swans, but they are anything but mute, hissing and honking endlessly. All the historical fuss over swan ownership was based on the fact that swans were once an important Royal food group. If this had continued to the present day, they would probably be serving McSwan sandwiches at the Windsor

McDonald's. Fortunately swans are *not* on the menu, but they do add to the atmosphere along the Thames at Windsor.

Lego Invades Windsor

When you visit Windsor Castle it is pretty hard to keep your children from learning that Legoland is only three miles down the road. We warned you that modern life has intruded on historic Windsor and there's no greater example of this than the Lego theme park.

You can go from the 900-year-old stones of Windsor Castle to the new plastic bricks of Legoland Windsor in about ten minutes via a shuttle bus that departs from both Windsor rail stations. The question is: do you want to? If you have a child under age ten who loves to play with Legos, this theme park will probably be a big hit. Older children may be disappointed because much of the park is geared toward younger kids. For example, the rides are pretty tame, especially by American theme park standards. But for the younger set, one favorite ride gives kids the chance to practice "driving" automobiles through an elaborate mock-up of city streets with traffic lights and signs. Chaos and fun ensues, especially for American children who have to adjust to British traffic rules. But the real jaw dropping sights for the true Lego fan (and his or her parents too) are the elaborate miniature European cities and landscapes built entirely from the plastic blocks. The model of London is phenomenal, although the cynic may point out the irony of paying to see a Lego model of London when the real thing is just a few miles away.

Legoland is a clean, well-run park designed to market the Lego brand, but don't expect any free product giveaways or reduced cost Legos for sale. While the gift shop has lots of Lego stuff, the prices are basically retail. In fact, some things cost more at Legoland than they do in American toy stores.

*　　　　　　*　　　　　　*

Where? When? £?

Windsor Castle

Location	The castle looms over the town of Windsor, located on the Thames west of London
Train	Trains travel from London's Paddington station to the town of Slough where you change trains for Windsor Central station. The journey takes about 35 minutes total and trains run every 20 minutes during much of the day. You can also take a train from London's Waterloo station to Windsor and Eton Riverside station. This avoids a change of trains, but the travel time is about 50 minutes. Both Windsor stations are walking distance to Windsor Castle.
Address	Windsor, Berkshire SL4 1NJ
Phone/email	020 7766 7304 bookinginfo@royalcollection.org.uk
Hours	March through October from 9:45 a.m. to 5:15 p.m. In other months, the castle closes at 4:15 p.m. Last admission is one hour before closing. Closed December 25-26. Parts of the castle can be closed when the Royals are in residence and for special events. St. George's Chapel is closed on Sundays.
Time Required	Two to four hours
Admission	Tickets are moderately priced. There are discounts for children, students, families, and seniors. Reduced admission when parts of the castle are closed. Tickets can be booked online.

Windsor Castle

Facilities	Self-service restaurant, tearoom. Outdoor picnic spots. Family play/restroom and baby-changing areas. Most areas are wheelchair accessible.
Website	www.royalcollection.org.uk

Where? When? £?

Frogmore House

Location	About a mile south of Windsor Castle in Windsor Home Park off the Long Walk
Address	Windsor Castle, Windsor, Berkshire SL4 1NJ
Phone/email	020 7766 7304 bookinginfo@royalcollection.org.uk
Hours	Very limited. Usually from 10:00 a.m. to 5:30 p.m. on the last weekend in August and 10:00 a.m. to 7:00 p.m. on one weekend in May. Mausoleum may also open on the Wednesday closest to May 24th (Queen Victoria's birthday) from 11:00 a.m. to 4:00 p.m. Days and hours may change.
Time Required	One hour
Admission	Tickets are reasonably priced. There are discounts for students and seniors.
Facilities	House is wheelchair accessible, but pathways are gravel
Website	www.royalcollection.org.uk

Where? When? £?

Legoland Windsor

Location	In Windsor, about 3 miles from Windsor Castle
Transportation	Shuttle bus from Windsor's train stations
Address	Winkfield Road, Windsor, Berkshire SL4 4AY
Phone/email	087 0504 0404 customerservices@legoland.co.uk
Hours	The park is open from late-March through October. The park opens at 10:00 a.m. and closes between 5:00 and 7:00 p.m. Check the website for details.
Time Required	Three to four hours
Admission	Tickets are expensive. There are discounts for children and seniors. Children under age three get in free. Tickets can be booked online.
Facilities	Many restaurants and snack bars onsite. Outdoor picnic spots. Toilets and baby-changing areas. Storage lockers and strollers (pushchairs) available for rent. Most areas are wheelchair accessible.
Website	www.legoland.co.uk

Off To Oxfordshire

Visitors to Windsor never really leave suburban London, but those who venture further northwest to Oxfordshire truly escape the city. Tourist agencies differ on where the heart of England lies, but if it is not quite England's heart, with Oxford University at its center, Oxfordshire may qualify as England's brain.

There are many reasons to visit here. The city of Oxford and its university is one obvious destination. Oxfordshire is also known as a gateway to the undeniably quaint Cotswolds region, and Stratford-Upon-Avon is just a few miles further northwest. But since our stated goal is to give just a taste of the region, we'll do that by describing two local attractions: the grandeur of Blenheim Palace and the mystery of the Rollright Stones.

Blenheim Palace

The year is 1704. What can a nobleman do to earn the absolute gratitude of England's Queen Anne? Why, defeat the French, of course. That's exactly what John Churchill did and Blenheim Palace was his reward. And some reward it was. Churchill, the first Duke of Marlborough, received the Royal Manor of Woodstock and the Queen's promise to pay for construction of Blenheim Palace. After falling out of royal favor, Churchill completed the grand palace at his own expense. In the years that followed, his descendants surrounded Blenheim with some of the country's most fantastic gardens.

If you travel around Britain for very long, grand palaces and stellar gardens become almost commonplace, but even to the veteran tourist Blenheim Palace is something special. Gazing at the exterior of

Blenheim Palace, it's hard not to start humming the theme music from *Masterpiece Theatre*. This is a palace of royal proportions, but it is also a private home. Inside, the grandeur and scale continue. The appropriately named Long Library, for example, is one of the longest rooms in any private home in England. The library contains thousands of books and one heck of a sound system—a cathedral-sized organ at one end of the vast room.

The Churchill name brings many visitors to Blenheim. The palace tour includes the room where Winston Churchill was born in 1874 and Churchill memorabilia and photographs are also on display. This is an ideal location to explain to your children the importance of Winston Churchill, perhaps linking the man to sights they have visited in London such as the Cabinet War Rooms. Kids may also be interested to learn that Churchill's mother was an American and that Winston Churchill was one of only a handful of people who have been granted honorary U.S. citizenship. Churchill's life comes full circle at his burial place in the nearby Oxfordshire town of Blanton.

The 2,000 acres of gardens and park that surround the palace are as impressive as the building itself. If Sir Christopher Wren was the architect of London's finest buildings, Lancelot "Capability" Brown was certainly the landscape architect of England's finest gardens. Blenheim Lake and the surrounding gardens are among Brown's grander works of landscape magic. Visiting families can rent rowboats here or take a motor launch trip on the lake.

Blenheim is no relic; the palace is still home to the current Duke of Marlborough and family. Upkeep on the palace and the surrounding park is not cheap, so the Duke has opened part of the palace to tourists and added some attractions to entice visitors. The latter may seem unnecessary to adults who are interested in seeing the landscape artistry of Capability Brown or visiting the birthplace of Winston Churchill. But for kids, the Duke's amusement park additions are great fun. So while you are touring the palace, promise your children a ride on the miniature train. While ogling the rose gardens, remind the kids they'll get to go through the palace's maze and play life-sized outdoor checkers and mini-golf (it's not as tacky as it sounds). Both children and adults will be interested in the Blenheim Butterfly House where exotic butterflies fly free in greenhouse-like enclosures.

Blenheim Palace is a fun place to visit and absorb some history, but only a few miles away on the Oxfordshire/Warwickshire border lies a more ancient and mysterious destination—the Rollright Stones.

In Search Of The Stones

Nearly everyone has heard of Stonehenge, but it comes as a surprise to many tourists that Britain is dotted with many other stone circles. Some are large and well-known, but there are a greater number of obscure stone circles lying literally in the middle of cow pastures. While the major sites have been excavated, x-rayed, and studied by scholars, the smaller stone circles are explained only by local legends.

The Rollright Stones are located in pastureland near the tiny Oxfordshire village of Long Compton not far from the town of Chipping Norton. After severely taxing our map reading skills, we managed to find this stone circle. The gatekeeper in his tiny shack charged our two children 20 pence admission to see the Rollright Stones, but he promised they could get the money back if they correctly counted the number of stones in the circle. The Rollright stone circle contains some very eroded stones and some that are nearly buried in the ground. In short, the actual number of stones was the subject of some debate. Each child reported back a different number to the gatekeeper who then informed them they were both wrong, but cheerfully refunded their 20 pence anyhow.

In the Oxfordshire fields, we learned several of the legends associated with the Rollright Stones. The best known story is documented back to at least the 1500s, so this is not something the locals recently made up at the village pub. (More likely they made it up at the pub 500 years ago.) It seems a king and his men were traveling through the area on their way to conquer all of England. They were intercepted by a local witch who made the king what seemed to be a great offer:

> "Seven long strides shalt thou take
> And if Long Compton thou canst see,
> King of England thou shalt be."

"Hot diggity" said the king as he strapped on his Nikes. No, that's wrong. What really happened was that the king started striding confidently across the field shouting:

> "Stick, stock, stone.
> As King of England I shall be known."

But the king did not count on the slight rise in the ground that blocked his view of the Long Compton village. After the king took his seventh step, the witch laughed and crowed "I'll get you my pretty, and your little dog too!" No, sorry for the confusion, these witch stories all sound alike. What she really said was:

> "As Long Compton thou canst not see
> King of England thou shalt not be.
> Rise up stick and stand still stone
> For King of England thou shalt be none;
> Thou and thy men hoar stones shall be
> And I myself an eldern tree."

This was the witch's way of turning the king into the King Stone that stands across the road from the Rollright Stones. The witch's spell changed the king's men into the nearby Kings Men Stone Circle. And with the last line of the spell, the witch went into retirement as an elder tree.

Stone Circles are not just the stuff of ancient legend. If you visit a stone circle during the summer solstice—the longest day of the year, usually around June 20th—you are often confronted with a *different* kind of fellow tourist. The first clue may be a number of old Volkswagen minibuses parked nearby or impromptu camp sites in surrounding fields. You won't confuse the solstice celebrators with other tourists by their clothing either: the fashion trend leans toward leftover 1968 counter-culture and the occasional druidical robe. Along the road near one isolated stone circle on the day of the summer solstice we noticed a long line of *no parking* signs and traffic cones. Near the field leading to the circle were two green National Trust vans and several uniformed men. They didn't give our family a second glance, but on the way out we stopped to talk with them. Careful not to offend, the National Trust rangers admitted that they were present to guard against an influx of "alternative" visitors. The previous year scads of people showed up to celebrate the solstice, overrunning the site and causing some damage. All we saw were a few regular tourists, but sure enough, as we drove away from the stone circle we came across a nearby campsite with a handful of solstice celebrators. Thus began an interesting conversation as we parents tried to explain who these unusual looking people were and why they were flocking to stone circles on the longest day of the year. The problem of solstice celebrations became so acute at Stonehenge that local authorities once closed off the site entirely on the summer solstice and now admit only limited numbers of solstice celebrators.

      *   *   *

Where? When? £?

Blenheim Palace

Location	At Woodstock, 8 miles north of Oxford on the A44 roadway (about 65 miles from London)
Transportation	Driving is easiest, but you can get a train from Paddington station in London to Oxford and take a bus from the Oxford Cornmarket to Blenheim Palace.
Address	Woodstock, Oxfordshire OX20 1PX
Phone	087 0060 2080
Hours	The palace is open daily from 10:30 a.m. to 5:30 p.m. from mid-February to the end of October. Also open Wednesday through Sunday from November through early December. Last admission to the palace is at 4:45 p.m. The park is open year round from 9:00 a.m. to 6:00 p.m. Closed on December 25.
Time Required	Three hours or longer
Admission	Tickets are moderately priced. There are discounts for children, students, seniors, and families. Costs are higher during spring and summer. Parks/gardens-only tickets available. Tickets may be booked online.
Facilities	Restaurant, cafés and picnic area onsite. Toilets and baby-changing areas. Some areas of palace and grounds are not wheelchair accessible.
Website	www.blenheimpalace.com

Where? When? £?

Rollright Stones

Location	Off the A3400 road, between Chipping Norton and the village of Long Compton on the Warwickshire/ Oxfordshire border, not far from Blenheim Palace and Oxford
Hours	Sunrise to sunset
Time Required	30 minutes to an hour
Admission	Ridiculously inexpensive
Facilities	None. Not wheelchair accessible.
Website	www.rollrightstones.co.uk

Baby, You Can Drive My Car

Country Churches

When you drive the back roads of rural Britain, allow time to stop and visit village churches, not necessarily as a religious experience, but for the history and local flavor that local churches provide. Churches were the focal point of village life in Britain, and they all have a story (usually explained in a 20 pence brochure sold inside the church).

Gustav Holtz was once the organist at the church in the tiny Cotswolds village of Wyck Rissington. He went on to fame as a composer of musical works such as *The Planets*. This historical side note was less fascinating to our children than the story of an elaborate maze formerly located near the village church. Fearing that it would be overrun by visitors, the builder razed it and only a mosaic plaque showing the maze remains on the church wall.

Church graveyards provide a resting place for the dead, but they can also serve as a temporary resting spot for the weary tourist. Ancient cemeteries are a good place to sit, reflect and absorb some of the quiet village atmosphere. The dead usually don't mind if you discretely munch a picnic snack while sitting quietly on a cemetery bench, reading stone inscriptions and contemplating their lives.

You will find another type of religious site in British towns and countryside. Literally hundreds of abbeys and cathedrals stand in ruined glory throughout Britain, a legacy of religious strife in the country's history. Try to visit at least one of these interesting ruins. Visit too many and your kids may begin to complain: "Geez, *another* old wrecked church?"

Now that we've whetted your appetite for a field trip, it is time to review some practical matters about traveling cross-country in Britain.

Hit The Road

Unless you have the nerves of a New York City taxicab driver, don't even think of driving in London. But if you are planning an extended trip outside the city, consider renting a midsize car or a minivan for exploring Britain. Fitting family luggage in the trunk of a small car can be difficult and a van allows kids room to sit by themselves and spread out their belongings and accumulated clutter. The visibility from a minivan is good enough that you can actually see over the hedgerows that border many of the rural roads. Of course, the convenience of a mid-sized car or van must also be balanced against the fuel economy of smaller vehicles. Fuel costs in Britain have historically been higher than in North America.

Car rental in Britain is not cheap, especially if you are looking for a family-sized vehicle. Consider arranging your rental before you leave the U.S. because local rental rates in Britain are often more expensive. In addition to contacting major car rental companies directly, check with your airline and with online car rental brokers. Before paying for optional collision insurance on a rental, check with your credit card company to see if coverage is automatically included when you charge the rental.

"Drive a car, on the wrong side of the road? You've got to be kidding!" is a common reaction from American tourists. Generally, driving on the left is less of a challenge than first imagined. It helps that the driver's seat is on the right, along with the appropriate controls. No the gas and brake pedals are not reversed, but the gearshift is on the left and that means shifting with your left hand, something which may just overtax your coping skills. Our strong recommendation is to rent a car with automatic transmission, despite the extra cost.

Once on the road, repeat this mantra: keep left, keep LEFT, KEEP LEFT! Actually, this is not overly difficult because everybody else is keeping left too—just follow them. Maybe the most difficult maneuver is turning right at an intersection and remembering to head for the left lane as you get on the next road (keep left, keep LEFT ...). Traffic circles ("roundabouts" in Britspeak) are very common, and are loads of fun for the tourist. Yield to the traffic in the circle—it will be coming from your right—but once you are in the circle, yield to no one. In a multi-lane roundabout, the outside lane is for immediate exits and the inner lanes are for those continuing further around the circle. Move left to exit out of the circle and use your turn signal to indicate whether you are turning out or staying in the roundabout. Miss your turn off? Just keep on going around the circle. Explaining this is harder than driving it, assuming you KEEP LEFT!

Driving in unfamiliar territory on the "wrong" side of the road is a lot easier if one adult navigates while the other drives. The keys here are to get good detailed maps, carefully plan your routes in advance, write down the directions, and keep your sense of humor. Just like in the U.S., driving the superhighways means missing much of the countryside and small towns. Britain's M roads are similar to American interstates. The more interesting routes are usually smaller A or B class roads, but, you'll definitely need good maps to negotiate the back roads. Where you have a choice, take the road that goes through an ancient village or requires a short ferryboat ride. You'll know you are on the scenic route when the road is narrower than your driveway back home.

Time And Distance

While England is a small country, we wonder sometimes whether the English mile is the same unit of measure as in the United States. Miles don't mean much in cities, where distances are usually measured in blocks, but while driving in the English countryside we once spotted a sign that read "Nottingham, 9 miles." The town was not on our planned itinerary, but it seemed a reasonable detour since the children wanted to see Sherwood Forest. We got off the M superhighway and started along smaller roads toward Nottingham. We drove, and drove, and drove some more before finally arriving in the legendary town about 40 minutes later. We concluded that traveling those nine miles fully explains the origins of the phrase "around Robin Hood's barn."

The lesson we have learned after driving thousands of miles on British roads is that the distance in miles may be small, but so are many of the roads. Once off the major highways, it is driving time, not distance, that matters most in planning your trip. Always allow extra driving time for contingencies like:

- Narrow, winding roads—our favorites in Cornwall were about 10 feet wide (total, for both lanes).

- Cattle and sheep crossings—this is a country where there are livestock crossings with flashing warning lights reminiscent of a school crossing back home.

- Roadwork—even on the smallest back country roads you will find "works" (but no flagmen/women; they use portable traffic signals at both ends of the project to direct traffic).

- Gypsy caravans—real gypsies, in colorful horse drawn wagons, going 3 miles per hour in a 45 miles per hour no passing zone.

- Unmarked roads—tiny roads that are usually signposted toward somewhere, but may not have a route number.

- Farm traffic—you haven't lived until you have followed a fertilizer wagon for a few fragrant, winding miles.

Train Wizardry

Arriving at Kings Cross rail station, Britain's most famous modern day wizard was as confused as any London tourist. To catch the Hogwarts Express train, Harry Potter searched the station for the elusive, invisible platform nine and three-quarters. While most "Muggle" travelers won't face this problem, Harry's experience proves that it pays to know what you are doing before walking into a London rail station.

With London as your base, trains let you add day trips to your visit. This gives your family a chance to broaden its horizons beyond London proper, even without renting a car and trying your hand at driving on the left. Some of the great places within an hour or two by train from London include close-in Windsor and Hampton Court, or more distance places like Bath, Oxford and York.

Rail travel works well with restless children since they can move around, look out the window, amuse other passengers, get a snack, and visit the loo … without stopping or slowing down progress toward your destination. Here are some tips to make train travel more comfortable, especially on longer trips:

- Round trip tickets are called return tickets in Britain. For day trips outside London, so-called cheap day return fares are often the best deals.

- Rail passes, such as the Britrail Pass, are generally a good deal if you are planning extensive rail travel in the United Kingdom. For a few day trips out of London a rail pass is not necessary or economical.

- Standard class seats are usually fine and first class accommodations are not worth the cost difference on most British railways.

- Do a little homework and try to sit on the side of the train with the best view. For example, if you are traveling on a coastal railway, sit on the side facing the water.

- Avoid the first few cars. Air pressure changes when entering tunnels can cause ear discomfort, particularly for young children.

- Some train cars are set up with four facing seats and a table between. Try to grab one of these so your kids can read, color, or eat a snack and you can easily keep tabs on them. But don't sit here if no one wants to ride facing backwards.

- Travelers can select cell phone-free cars on some trains. You may appreciate the peace and quiet.

- Many rail stations don't have lifts (elevators). If you and your children can't carry your luggage up and down stairs, then you have a real problem. Most stations have luggage carts, but no porters, and carts are useless on stairways. Friendly strangers have occasionally helped our family with luggage, but you may not be so lucky. Allow plenty of extra time to lug that luggage or risk missing your train. In London, the main rail stations are all on one level, or they have lifts, so luggage toting is not a big problem here. However, some London Underground/Tube stations do not have lifts or escalators.

- Some smaller stations in the countryside are fully automated with electronic ticket vending machines and computer screens that announce arrivals and departures. This can be disconcerting to the tourist whose inclination is to look for an information counter to ask questions. With a little practice, and adequate time before your train departs, the automated system works well.

- Consider train travel as another picnic opportunity since the food served on trains is not that great and it can be expensive.

- British railway employees sometimes go on strike, disrupting rail service. That's a real problem for the tourist who has to get around on a schedule and can't just hop in the family automobile if the trains are not running. However, in a civilized British manner, the rail strikes are sometimes scheduled for specific days so you can plan around them.

The British rail system has been privatized, resulting in some reductions in service as well as some rail system improvements. Changes are continuing, so it is wise to use only up-to-date information when planning a train trip in Britain.

Rail Station Roulette

When railway travel got its start in Britain, London responded by building rail stations—lots of them—all over the city. There's no Grand Central station in London. Instead, the traveler is faced with over a dozen major train stations scattered throughout town. Like the spokes in a wheel, the rail lines from each station reach out and serve different parts of Britain. Major stations include:

- Paddington
- Marylebone
- Euston
- St. Pancras
- Kings Cross
- Liverpool Street
- Fenchurch Street
- Blackfriars
- Charing Cross
- Cannon Street
- London Bridge
- Waterloo
- Victoria

With the exception of St. Pancras and Kings Cross, which are right across the street from each other, getting from one station to another can be a real pain. The Tube is not really practical if you're carrying much luggage. London's bus system indirectly connects rail stations, but this is not ideal either. Taxis are probably the most practical, if expensive, ways to get between rail stations in London. Try to avoid rush hours because whatever conveyance you choose—bus, taxi, or Tube—it takes longer when London's streets are jammed.

Train travel in London sounds like a nightmare? Fortunately, most tourists will probably only use one or two of the rail stations, either to get into London from an airport, or to take a day trip outside the city. The list below shows examples of popular rail destinations, some of the London stations that serve them, and the approximate journey time. Remember, rail services can change, so check with the official National Rail website.

Destination	Train leaves from	Travel time
Gatwick Airport	Victoria	30 minutes
Heathrow Airport	Paddington	15 minutes
Bath	Paddington	90 minutes
Oxford	Paddington	1 hour
Windsor	Paddington or Waterloo	35-50 minutes
Cambridge	Kings Cross	1 hour
York	Kings Cross	2 hours
Edinburgh	Kings Cross	$4\frac{1}{2}$ hours
Paris, France	St. Pancras	Under 3 hours

Train Times And Tickets

Tickets can be purchased at rail stations, or even once you are onboard, but advance planning will save time and money. For schedules, station information, and purchases see the semi-official Transport Direct website at www.transportdirect.info. Using the Transport Direct site you can enter destinations and departure points, dates and times of travel and get online schedules. This site also provides links to railway operating companies, updates on schedule disruptions, locations of rail stations, and other information.

        *   *   *

PART 4

Stop Dreaming, Start Planning

When To Go?

Don't you just love this section in the typical guidebook? Parents with school-age children generally *can't* go to London in September or October even though the weather may be beautiful. And most kids would throw a fit if you decided to pack up and go to London for Christmas or another important holiday: "What about the presents? How will Santa Claus find me?" So yes, it's great to contemplate going to Britain at some other time of year, but most families will travel during the summer months of June, July, or August.

Now that we've had a reality check, is there any way to travel in the summer but miss the crowds? One trick is to avoid the times when British schools are on summer break. Fortunately, British schools usually get out for the summer in early-to-mid July, while most American schools end in June, giving American families a window of opportunity for travel. During this period you'll still encounter crowds, but hopefully not the crush which can occur in some parts of Britain during summer school holidays. The impact is greatest in holiday spots favored by the natives, such as coastal areas in Cornwall and Devon. Crowding in London during the summer is usually caused by foreign tourists who swarm into the city in August.

Travelers to London will feel the mid-summer crunch on the plane trip over (no empty seats where kids can stretch out and get some sleep), at the airport (customs and immigrations lines can be endless), and at major tourist attractions in the city (lines to see the crown jewels are notorious).

Some airlines hike fares for summer travel beginning on or about June 15th, so if you can manage to begin your trip before the rates go up, you can save a little money. On the other hand, airlines sometimes offer summer fare sales, depending upon competitive pressures, often announcing them in April or later. This can be a Catch-22: wait too long and all the early June flights will be filled; book too early and you won't know if a summer sale will be available.

Rates at hotels which cater primarily to business travelers don't necessarily increase in summer. In fact, you may find summer price breaks at London's business hotels and weekend rates at such hotels can also be lower.

Holidays

Just in case you go to London at some time other than the summer, here is a list of the major public holidays observed in Britain throughout the year:

Holiday	Date observed
New Year's Day	January 1. If a weekend, the holiday is next weekday.
Good Friday	Varies
Easter Monday	Varies
Early May Bank Holiday	First Monday in May
Spring Bank Holiday	Last Monday in May
Summer Bank Holiday	Last Monday in August
Christmas Day	December 25. If a weekend, the holiday is the next weekday after Boxing Day.
Boxing Day	December 26

Bank holiday is a quaint term designating an official holiday when banks and other places of business are closed. Be sure and check to see whether the tourist attractions you want to visit are open on a holiday.

Many are closed around Christmas and New Year's, but open on other holidays.

Weather

Going to Britain in summer means you can expect the following weather conditions: warm, hot, cool, cold, sunny, cloudy, and wet. Sometimes these all occur in one day! Here's a table showing average high and low temperatures by month in London:

Month	Low	High
January	36°F	43°F
February	36°	44°
March	38°	50°
April	42°	56°
May	47°	62°
June	53°	69°
July	56°	71°
August	56°	71°
September	52°	65°
October	46°	58°
November	42°	50°
December	38°	45°

Average temperatures are derived from *years* of actual data so you could experience a hot or cold spell during the relatively few days of your visit, regardless of the averages. Use the averages as a guide, but pack something to wear if you encounter un-average temperatures. There has been a recent trend towards unusual summer heat waves in London and southern England as global climate changes impact Britain.

A real bonus to traveling in late June is that as you approach summer solstice the days get long—really long—at this latitude. Twilight lasts past 10:00 p.m. in London, and as you travel north to the English Lake District or Scotland, there is still a little light in the western sky at 11:30 p.m. This gives the summer tourist some extra hours of sightseeing time in the evenings. British summer time (daylight savings time) starts on the last Sunday of March and ends on the last Sunday of October. Note that the longer days don't necessarily mean extended opening times for tourist sights, but you can use the longer daylight hours for outdoor activities.

A Method To Your Trip Planning Madness

It is amazing how many families do almost no research before taking an overseas trip. This method works fine sometimes, but serendipitous tourists may miss some great experiences simply because they did not have enough information before arriving in Britain.

The solution? If you have the luxury of time, start planning six months or more before your trip. Buy or borrow every guidebook you can find (borrow others, *buy* this one please), split them up among family members, and just start reading. Take notes about things that interest you, then swap books and take more notes. Go online and search for sites related to travel, tourism, dining, events and lodging in Britain. Contact VisitBritain.com, the British tourism agency, for information and maps. Take a look at VisitLondon.com, the official London tourism website.

If you want your kids to "buy into" a trip consider involving them in planning it. Start by sharing guidebooks and interesting, appropriate websites. Then give your children a map and let them mark sights, hotels, and points of interest. In the time leading up to your trip, point out news about Britain in newspapers, magazines and on television. Mention some of the many American historical connections to Britain—George Washington's parents, the Pilgrims, Sir Walter Raleigh, Ben Franklin—and how these are related to subjects your children have studied in school. Encourage your kids to read some British children's literature, especially stories that take place in areas you will visit.

When you and your children cannot read another guidebook, brochure, or *Paddington Bear* story, it's time for a family conference.

Everyone contributes from their notes and you begin to develop a master list of places and things you want to see and do and some idea of where you want to stay. Narrowing this list down to a trip plan is step two—and this is no small challenge. At this point, independent travelers will begin contacting airlines and hotels directly. People who find this prospect too daunting may decide it's time to "punt" and turn to a travel agent for help.

If you use an agent, be sure to pick one with extensive, recent travel experience in Britain. Any travel agent can sell packaged tours, but it takes much more knowledge for an agent to answer your questions about specific hotels, sights, and other aspects of your trip. Beware of anyone—travel agent or guidebook writer—who strongly steers you toward a particular hotel (or airline, car rental agency, etc.). They could be providing you their best impartial, factual advice, or there could be an ulterior economic motive behind the recommendation.

Laying Out An Itinerary
—The Block Planning Method

You've read extensively, taken copious notes, bookmarked lots of internet sites, and have loads of brochures and guidebooks piled on the dining room table. How do you organize all this information into a trip plan? Our suggestion is to use what we call the *block planning method*. Simply lay out the days of your trip like a weekly personal organizer calendar, with enough room to write in places to visit and special events for your trip. Take your "want to do" list and start blocking out possible times on the calendar. Some suggestions:

- First, fill in anything that is fixed, such as arrival and departure dates and times. If you have pre-purchased theater tickets, fill in the show times on the calendar. Add any special one-time events you wish to attend.

- Plan for variety by mixing and matching types of activities. Don't put all the museums on one day and all the parks on another. The wise parent carefully intersperses kid-friendly activities between the more adult (possibly kid-boring) events.

- Block out enough time for each sight or activity. This book tries to give you some idea about how long you may spend at certain places, but this is just our best estimate. You may want to devote more or less time, but when planning, err on the side of leaving yourself extra time. And remember, it also takes time to get from place to place.

- Consider geography. Arrange your visit logically, grouping sights and events that are reasonably close together. Plot your itinerary out on a map and if your routes look like a web spun by a drunken spider, you may want to rearrange a little.

- Be flexible. Have some backups if you plan to visit a park and it rains, or if the lines at some sights are too long.

- Be realistic. As a rule of thumb, when traveling with children, you can probably do three major activities a day: one each in the morning, afternoon, and evening. Too much more and your kids will be exhausted, too little and they may be bored.

Laying this all out graphically is the best way we know to get a handle on family trip plans. Of course, once you get it down on paper or in a spreadsheet, you'll probably change it several times before you leave for Britain (and several times after you are there).

Don't Leave Home Without The Book

As your plans firm up, we suggest creating a three-ring notebook that includes:

- Your block plan itinerary.
- Photocopies of the photograph page from your family's passports (if you lose a passport, the copy can help speed up getting a replacement).
- Copies of hotel reservation confirmations.
- Photocopies of airline tickets, theater tickets, museum passes, rental car reservations.
- Phone numbers to report lost credit cards.
- Photocopies of a few pages from those huge guidebooks which you don't want to lug around Britain. Two suggestions: copy only pages from books you own and use the copies only for personal use while on the trip. Don't deliberately violate copyright laws, but if the alternative is to cut pages out of your books....

Since you have to carry this thousands of miles, use the smallest width notebook that will hold your information. Use a binder with pockets in the front and back and insert maps there.

Just how valuable is The Book? It has literally saved our vacation when faced with a balky hotel, airline, or car rental reservation. "Sorry sir, we have no record of *that* low rate" or "We never promise a vehicle with automatic transmission" can be instantly met with your retort "Well, as you can see from my copy of your email confirmation here ..." as you extract the documentation from The Book.

Events

Events, big and small, planned and serendipitous, can make a trip special. Your goal as the intrepid tourist is to take advantage of special events that you know about in advance *and* to be flexible enough to enjoy those unplanned moments when events find you.

On one trip, we had arranged far in advance for tickets to the Ceremony of the Keys at the Tower of London. What we didn't know until we arrived in London was that we were attending the ceremony on the same night as the 100th anniversary celebration for nearby Tower Bridge. After the solemn keys ceremony, we literally ran to the embankment of the Thames and watched spectacular fireworks above Tower Bridge. That was serendipity at its best.

In some cases, you may want to avoid special events—if you know about them—especially occasional protest marches and rallies which spill out of Hyde Park and can clog central London. You normally don't need to fear riot police and tear gas, because for the most part, the British stage rather civilized protest marches. On one visit to London, we encountered a gay pride rally and had an interesting time explaining some of the elaborately dressed marchers to our young son.

When you arrive in London, get a copy of the publication *Time Out London* for up-to-date information on events and activities.

Finding A Hotel

When considering where to stay, check as many sources as you can. Read through guidebooks and surf lodging websites for accommodations that are convenient to central London. Find a great place? What does the AA (British Automobile Association) guide or website say? Can you find the same hotel listed in the Michelin Guide or any of the numerous lodging guides covering Britain? Go online again and see what people are saying on travel message boards or services like TripAdvisor.com. Find out if the hotel has a website; it will be biased, but a website may provide photographs of the hotel, maps showing its exact location, and other useful information. Remember, a palace to one person may be a pigsty to someone else. Do not rely on any one source when deciding where to stay—lest you end up sleeping in a pigsty, or worse.

Even with many sources of information, families traveling to London face several challenges in finding suitable lodging. We have some suggestions, but no outright solutions, to finding:

- family accommodations;
- a quiet, comfortable place to stay;
- a convenient location; and
- something you can afford.

Family Rooms

The typical American hotel room contains two double/queen beds, a modern full bathroom, and air-conditioning. A family of two adults and one or two children can usually fit into this configuration, perhaps with a rollaway bed for one child. It's not paradise, especially for the parents, but it suffices. For a few dollars more a traveling family in North America can stay at an all-suite hotel chain in relative comfort and privacy.

This American model rarely applies to the British hotel industry and it is sometimes difficult to find modern, family accommodations in Britain. But in London, one possibility is to try a familiar brand hotel like Holiday Inn, Hilton or Marriott. Kids usually stay free with their parents in a typical, American-style hotel room. Some British hotel chains, such as the budget-minded Travel Inn, also offer familiar-style accommodations in London. But even at brand name hotels, make no assumptions. Check with the individual hotel before you make a reservation and take time to learn the euphemisms employed in the hotel industry. The word "traditional" often means old, a "tourist class hotel" is a lower grade property, and "first class" is not necessarily the top of the line. Modifiers are sometimes used to denote middle range hotels, so you may see a "moderate first class" hotel or a "superior tourist class" property.

Triple, quad, or family rooms do exist in London hotels, they are just hard to find. But if you've added other criteria, such as air-conditioning and a central London location, family rooms are even rarer. In a traditional tourist class or moderate first class hotel a family room is likely to be four single beds in a slightly larger than normal hotel room. Modern, reasonably priced suite hotels, which are popular in the United States, are uncommon in London.

There have been changes in the moderately priced London hotel scene. The Travel Inn hotel chain has expanded into central London, offering reasonably priced hotels right downtown. Travel Inn hotels feature modern, nonsmoking rooms including some family bedrooms. Travel Inns do not have air-conditioning, however. One Travel Inn is in County Hall, near the London Eye and just across the river from Parliament; another is near Tower Bridge. Travel Inn and its competitors are making inroads with the tourist trade at the expense of older traditional London hotels.

Quiet, Please!

Finding an air-conditioned hotel in London is a challenge. If you visit in the summer though, you'll probably want air-conditioning. Not because London is normally hot—it isn't, especially compared to many areas in North America. The reason for air-conditioning is noise control. London is a very busy city and if your hotel room is anywhere near a major street, a nightclub, a taxi stand, a theater, or a trash dumpster you'll want to be able to keep the windows closed. In warm weather, without air-conditioning, the hotel guest is faced with a choice of no sleep because of noise outside an open window, or no sleep because the room is stuffy and warm with the window closed.

The need for quiet is one reason to look at the newer hotel chains. Their construction tends to include double-glazed windows, carpeting, some sound insulation, and quieter plumbing. Be sure to check, even some new hotels in London are not air-conditioned.

Our preference for modern, air-conditioned hotels may not be yours. If you prefer small, older hotels or B&Bs you may be able to find something that will suit your needs, but it will take some research to find quiet, quality rooms. Lodging guidebooks may associate "quiet" with "no children allowed." For families, quiet means the possibility of a good night's sleep, not the quiet of a nursing home. Of course nothing guarantees a quiet hotel or B&B. Ever notice that fellow hotel guests seem to practice slamming their room doors after 11:00 p.m.? It is these same people who think that a hotel hallway is a fine place to hold loud, protracted conversations late at night or first thing in the morning.

Locating a hotel on a large scale London map can often give you some clues about potential noise from road traffic. A hotel facing busy Piccadilly or Kensington Road is going to be exposed to more traffic noise than someplace just a block off the main road. No guarantees here either, however, since the hotel could be right next to the *Party All Night Pub* or some equally loud venue.

Unfortunately, there sometimes seems to be an inverse relationship between a quiet hotel and one with a good central location (our next criteria).

Location, Location, Location

London has good public transportation, so getting from a distant hotel to the major tourist sights is certainly possible. But do you really want to spend valuable vacation time traveling on the Tube, with children in tow, during the morning rush hour? Wouldn't it be better to stay near some of the sights you want to see?

This distinction escapes many experts who advise tourists to look for reasonably priced lodgings that cluster in some remote areas of London. Before you start the process of deciding on a specific hotel, grab a London city map and let us take you on a tour of some of the city's neighborhoods. We'll let you know the kinds of lodging you can expect to find, some pros and cons of staying in each spot, and some observations about how convenient the neighborhoods are to the major tourist sights.

Find Buckingham Palace on the map. The Palace will serve as the center of an imaginary clock face we use to describe the city's regions. Our overview starts in the Paddington and Bayswater areas, at 10:00 on the clock, just north of Kensington Gardens. We will work anti-clockwise (that's Britspeak for counter-clockwise). In addition to the clock analogy, we have included a main postal code for each area to help you locate it on a London map.

Paddington and **Bayswater** (postal code W2) are home to lots of lower cost hotels, including many tourist class accommodations that are used by package tour operators. Bayswater is a multi-cultural area with a number of small shops and ethnic restaurants, but unfortunately most of the Bayswater area is not close to major tourist sights, so you have to rely on the Tube, buses or taxis to get to these areas. One advantage of the Paddington/Bayswater area is that it is very convenient for people arriving and departing by train from and to Heathrow Airport since the Paddington rail station is the London terminus for the Heathrow Express train service to Heathrow. If rail convenience is paramount, there is a Hilton Hotel connected to the Paddington rail station. Bayswater Road, just south of the Bayswater area, runs along the top of Kensington Gardens and Hyde Park. Hotels at the eastern end of this road (near Marble Arch) tend to be somewhat more upscale than those in Bayswater proper.

Moving back to 8:30 on our imaginary clock, you come to **Earl's Court** (postal code SW5), another place where there is a cluster of mid-priced lodgings. But Earl's Court is actually further away from most tourist sights than Bayswater.

Moving inward from Earl's Court, is **Kensington** (postal code W8), an area just below the gardens of the same name. This region has a number of hotels and it is a little closer to the core tourist sights, especially at its eastern end (the **Knightsbridge** area). Kensington is also very convenient for visiting Kensington Palace and Gardens as well as the Science, Natural History, and Victoria and Albert museums. Kensington Road is extremely busy (with requisite traffic noise) but there are some quieter side streets south of this thoroughfare.

Trendy **Chelsea** (postal code SW3) is about 7:00 on our London clock. This area is home to B&Bs, boutique hotels, and some large high-priced hotels. Lovely as it is, Chelsea attracts young, upscale residents, but few major tourist sights are located here.

Victoria rail station is just below Buckingham Palace, close in and at 6:00 in our clock analogy (postal code SW1). Victoria is near enough that you can easily walk to the palace and many other central sights. This neighborhood includes some grimy locations, as well as a few nicer spots, so choose carefully. Some Victoria area hotels are older tourist class establishments used by package tour operators.

The **Westminster Abbey** area is at 3:00 on our clock. Unfortunately, there are relatively few hotels in this part of Westminster (postal code SW1). It would be nice to stay so close to the Abbey, Parliament, and other important locations, but the real estate here is pretty high-priced and so are many of the local hotels. One exception is a moderately priced Fullers Inn just south of St. James's Park. Across the river from Parliament and literally next door to the London Eye, the old London County Hall has been converted into shops, restaurants, an aquarium, and hotels. There is a moderately priced Travel Inn here along with an expensive Marriott.

At about 2:00 on the clock tour, and within walking distance of Buckingham Palace, is the ritzy **St. James's** area (also postal code SW1). The hotels in this area are among the most central, and the most expensive, in the city. The Stafford Hotel is tucked into a quiet St. James's side street and offers upscale accommodations befitting the area. St. James's is often lumped with Mayfair, its northern neighbor, as a locale for upscale accommodations. A bit further out from the center at the 2:00 position is the **Covent Garden** area (postal code WC2). This neighborhood is convenient to the theaters of the West End as well as the attractions in and around Covent Garden Market. Theaters and the festival atmosphere of Covent Garden can mean traffic and late night noise outside your hotel window.

Continuing back around the clock to the 1:00 position and moving out a little farther from the center, you come to **Bloomsbury** (postal code WC1). Bloomsbury is near the British Museum, but not much else on the typical tourist's agenda. While it is too far to walk from here to many of London's central sights, Bloomsbury does boast a number of moderately priced hotels.

Near 12:00 on our imaginary clock are three contiguous areas with concentrations of hotels. Far out the clock's hand is the **Regent's Park** neighborhood (postal code NW1). You can stay here in luxury at the upscale Langham Hotel. Regent's Park is close to the zoo, Regent's Canal, and a few tourist sights, but it takes a Tube or taxi ride to get to the center of London. Below Regent's Park, but north of Oxford Street, is the **Marylebone** area (also postal code NW1). Marylebone is convent to shopping along Oxford Street, and it has good access to the Tube, but it's still a long walk to the center of our clock/map.

On the south side of Oxford Street is **Mayfair** (postal code W1). You can't get much more convenient than Mayfair, but convenience comes at a price. The hotels, shops, and restaurants here tend to be very expensive, although there are a few chain hotels in which you can obtain more reasonable rooms. They are still expensive, just not outrageously so. A popular mid-range choice is the Holiday Inn Mayfair, just across the street from the over-the-top luxury of The Ritz. The Chesterfield Mayfair hotel, further north into Mayfair, offers a bit more luxury, but not at Ritz levels or prices.

To the east of our imaginary clock face is the **City** (postal codes EC3, EC4). The City is convenient to a group of important tourist destinations including St. Paul's Cathedral, the Tower of London, Tower Bridge—and it is just across the river from the Globe Theatre and other south bank sights. Although the City is primarily a financial district, there are a number of hotels within walking distance of tourist sights that may be worth considering. Some new hotels have been built on the South Bank of the Thames and are still relatively convenient to the City. Further east, new hotels have sprouted in **Canary Wharf** and **East London** concurrent with redevelopment in these areas.

Location is undeniably important, but unfortunately, an inverse relationship sometimes exists between location and affordability (our next criteria).

And That Will Be £300, Plus VAT And Service Charges

We promised to address four issues at the start of this section and we have delivered on the first three: we've discussed finding family accommodations, given some hints on getting a quiet hotel room, and provided an overview of hotel locations. About the last issue—finding affordable places to stay—can we take a rain check?

Seriously, it is tempting to skip this subject because of one simple fact: lodging in London is expensive. Lodging which also meets all the criteria we've outlined is both difficult to find *and* expensive. We do not claim to have magic answers, but we can offer some more suggestions.

Never Say Never

First, wherever you travel, never accept the published hotel rate at a large city hotel. You will always qualify for some lower rate: weekend packages, honeymoon packages (kind of hard to explain when you're traveling with kids), government rates, corporate rates, automobile association rates, senior citizen rates, special rates for people paying with a particular credit card, *something*. If nothing else works, and you are planning to stay at a chain hotel, find out if you can get a better rate by joining their frequent guest program.

Most major hotel chains have toll-free telephone reservations services or internet sites, but if you call an American-based central reservations service for a chain hotel, they may be woefully uninformed about the details of their London properties. We've been told by the reservations service that a London hotel has no family rooms, only to contact the hotel directly and find out that family rooms are available. It takes some persistence, but usually you can reserve a family room through the reservations service. Ask the reservations clerk to contact the hotel directly about family rooms if nothing appears on the reservations computer system. A lot depends upon the helpfulness and persistence of the individual reservations agent. We were lucky to work with one such agent for a large hotel chain who negotiated two adjoining rooms at a discounted rate even though the chain's computer system did not include special rates for family accommodations. Web-based reservations systems often aren't much better if you are trying to book family rooms or connecting rooms.

Like most large cities, London has hotels that cater primarily to business travelers and these hotels may have lower rates on weekends than during the week. While you will probably stay longer than a weekend, make sure you get the lower rate for at least the weekend portion of your stay. You can also take advantage of off-peak times at business-oriented London hotels. Happily, off-peak for business travel is July and August which is exactly when many families go to London on vacation.

Call Around

Sometimes you can find lower rates by calling a hotel directly. Take this a step further and compare rates quoted by the hotels, their corporate reservations centers, and websites. Look in travel magazines and in those tiny ads in the Sunday newspaper travel section, check with airlines, and surf the many travel sites available on the internet. Bidding on a travel auction site is another way to obtain lower-cost accommodations, but travel auctions are not for everyone. It can be difficult to arrange family rooms, adjoining rooms, or any special configurations via an auction.

A word of caution though. Be sure you are comparing apples to apples. Are the rooms the same? Some hotels have several grades of accommodation, including both recently refurbished accommodations and some pretty shabby rooms. Does the quoted rate include:

- Value Added Tax (it should);
- service charges; and
- breakfasts or any meals (for the whole family or just two adults)?

Make sure the rates are quoted on the same basis: per room, per night. Do children stay free and, if so, are there age limits? Finally, make certain you know whether the rate is quoted in dollars or pounds. It sounds basic, but there have been some very nasty surprises for tourists who neglected to find this out in advance.

Quality Ratings

Sherlock Holmes would be quite comfortable searching for a decent place to stay in London, applying his powers of deductive reasoning, using his able assistant Watson and examining clues under a magnifying glass. Holmes would have made a terrific trip planner since he seemed to have a lot of free time on his hands and no real money worries.

Fortunately, Sherlock, someone has done a lot of detective work already. The English Tourist Board and the Automobile Association each rate thousands of hotels, B&Bs, and other lodging establishments in Britain. The Tourist Board has worked to establish a standard set of criteria, along with a simple rating system—awarding one to five stars or diamonds based on standards of quality, services offered, and facilities. Generally, the more stars or diamonds, the better the hotel or B&B, but there are differences. A hotel is graded with a heavy emphasis on its facilities—things like bathrooms, elevators, and room service. A bed and breakfast is evaluated more in terms of quality and "helpful friendly service." To qualify for two stars a hotel has to provide *ensuite* or private bathrooms and color televisions in all bedrooms; to receive a single diamond rating, B&Bs must offer a full cooked breakfast and adequate heating and hot water (plus a dose of that helpful friendly service, we presume). To further qualify the ratings, the Tourist Board doles out gold and silver awards and the AA gives red stars and a quality percentage score. So the simplified standards are not as simple as they appear. Furthermore, if you plan to stay in a self-catering accommodation (a rental cottage), there is another star rating system.

From an American perspective, where even inexpensive hotel rooms come with phones, TVs, air-conditioning, and private baths, it's a little disconcerting to read these standards. "Bathrooms down the hall? They've got to be kidding!" Well tourist, you're not in Kansas anymore.

In practice, take all rating systems with a grain of salt. One of the nicest places we've stayed in Britain was a beautiful B&B in the tiny west coast village of Crackington Haven. The B&B owners had dropped out of the voluntary Tourist Board inspection program, claiming that the Board emphasized facilities at the expense of quality. So while you undoubtedly want heat and hot water, you may not need all the facilities which constitute a four or five diamond establishment, especially if you are staying in a small B&B.

The Flat Alternative

Families staying a week or longer in London may want to consider renting a flat (an apartment) as an alternative to staying in a hotel. Flats come in all sizes and quality levels, and the better ones cost every bit as much as a good hotel room. What a flat offers families is often more space, perhaps even separate rooms for children and adults, and kitchen facilities in which to prepare some meals. Groceries in London are not cheap, but fixing a few meals in your flat is still less expensive than constantly eating in restaurants.

Many rental flats tend to be located in residential areas away from major tourist sights. As long as they are reasonably close to a Tube or suburban rail station, it is fairly easy to commute into central London, but this does add commuting logistics to your visit. Finding a quiet, comfortable flat may take more research—and more faith—than finding a suitable hotel room. Some factors to consider:

- Is the flat air-conditioned? (Fat chance!)
- Is the building new, renovated, or "classic"?
- Are there lifts (elevators)?
- How convenient is the flat to what you want to see in London? Is it near a Tube stop?
- What is the neighborhood like?
- Is there a grocery store nearby?

There are a number of agencies that specialize in short term flat rentals in London. Check the internet, advertisements in travel magazines, or the travel sections of major newspapers. Renting a flat while on vacation is often a lifestyle choice. Do you want to mingle with the natives, shop for food and fix meals? Do you have the time to devote to domestic chores during your stay?

B&Bs, Country Hotels And Inns

Families traveling outside of London may have an easier time finding a quiet, comfortable, affordable place to stay. There are many options: bed and breakfasts, country house hotels, inns, traditional hotels, and (in some locations) modern chain hotels.

You can't go very far anywhere in Britain without seeing a B&B. In central London, B&Bs are less common, but they exist in some neighborhoods. The term "bed and breakfast" covers a lot of ground. It applies to families who rent out one or two bedrooms in their homes and to larger establishments which are essentially small hotels. But virtually all B&Bs share one characteristic: the ubiquitous English breakfast (see the *Food, Glorious Food* section).

Country house hotels are a cross between a rural B&B and a hotel. Generally they have more rooms and are usually upscale establishments, located in the countryside. Most visitors to London will not stay in a country hotel unless they choose to stay far outside the city and commute in by train.

The term *inn* often implies a small establishment that rents rooms and has a restaurant that is open to non-residents. In some cases, the presence of a pub or restaurant where you are staying can add an element of noise as diners arrive, eat, drink, and be merry late into the night. Most inns are located in smaller towns and villages—they are not common in London.

The quality of B&Bs, country house hotels, and inns varies from simple to luxurious. A more subjective factor—charm—also varies from "working class spare bedroom" to "country squire's guest villa." It takes some detective work to determine an establishment's charm factor sight unseen. The process is just like finding a hotel in London: get hold of every reference source you can find and start cross-checking.

One debate among travelers to Britain is whether to reserve B&B rooms in advance, or simply find them as you travel from place to place. With children in tow, finding suitable accommodations can be challenging. A traveling family can't be as flexible as two traveling adults since younger children need beds in the same room with parents (or very nearby). Add the fact that not all B&Bs accept children and you have a strong case for making advance reservations. If you choose the serendipitous method, local tourist information centers are a good source for finding B&Bs as you go.

Once you've narrowed down the choices, call, fax or email the places you want to stay. If you decide to call, keep the time differential in mind and also try to avoid calling during the busy breakfast period or late in the evening. You'll discover that most B&B owners are very helpful, and you can ask those questions that guidebooks may not cover. We always find a tactful way to ask whether the B&B is really in the quiet country-side, or if it is located just a few feet from a busy highway. Impolite? Hey, it beats being surprised when you get there!

A note about B&B prices—they are usually quoted per person, not per room. Children generally do not stay free, in fact they often pay the same rate as adults.

Despite all your research, it is hard to know what your selected B&B or hotel will really be like. We have made reservations at places that sounded fantastic, and were disappointed when we arrived. We've made reservations at B&Bs that sounded ordinary, and have been pleasantly surprised. We have gone without reservations and found wonderful places on the fly ... there are few guarantees here.

Sleep well!

Food, Glorious Food

Paddington eyed the tray hungrily. There was half a grapefruit in
a bowl, a plate of bacon and eggs, some toast, and a whole pot of
marmalade, not to mention a large cup of tea. "Is all that for
me?" he exclaimed.

—from *A Bear Called Paddington* by Michael Bond

It's a fact of life for parents traveling with young children: meals can be
a real challenge. In London this challenge is compounded by other facts:
the food is not always terrific, but it can be terrifically expensive.

Many traditional London guidebooks extol the modern dining renaissance that has occurred in London. To some degree they are right
because the stereotypical dreary British cuisine of old has vastly
improved in this cosmopolitan city. That's terrific news for wealthy,
vacationing adults who can go to all the chic new restaurants and experience nouvelle British cuisine. But realistically, families traveling to
London are hard-pressed to share in this upscale culinary renaissance.
Fortunately, there is a trickle-down effect with better food available
from less pricey brasseries, restaurant chains and even sandwich shops.
Still, it can sometimes be a challenge to find reasonably priced meals,
with food and atmosphere acceptable to both adults and children.

Full English Breakfast

If you're lucky, breakfast is included with your hotel room. All B&Bs
include breakfast—that's the reason for the second "B"—and many
hotels follow suit. English breakfasts come in two basic varieties: conti-

nental and full English. If your kids normally survive on cereal, the continental breakfast may suffice. Depending upon the establishment, a continental breakfast may include some type of puffed rice cereal, maybe corn flakes, and muesli—the European cereal favorite. If your kids must have chocho-kicko-snappy pops, or some other nutritious American breakfast cereal, they may be out of luck. In some places, however, a continental breakfast is simply bread, jam, coffee and tea.

The full English breakfast is a heavy tradition in Britain. Heavy on eggs (served fried unless you ask for them another way), heavy on bacon or sausage, heavy on toast and jam. And as a bonus, the full English breakfast often comes with broiled mushrooms and broiled tomatoes. Not that there is anything nutritionally wrong with mushrooms or tomatoes, but the first time they are served at breakfast be prepared for strange looks or inappropriate comments from your children. Sometimes, the British go even further and offer baked beans as a breakfast side dish. This is the point where many Americans draw the line in the cultural sand. Here's our read on full English breakfasts:

- Day 1—"Boy, these eggs and ham are great. What's with these broiled tomatoes and mushrooms?"
- Day 2—"Wow, another big breakfast. Good thing we're doing so much walking."
- Day 3—"No thanks, I'll pass on the baked beans."
- Day 4—"I wonder how much cholesterol is in this?"
- Day 5 through the end of the trip—"I don't ever want to see a broiled tomato or mushroom again."

The Brown Bag Solution

One solution for feeding the family is to buy a soft-sided insulated picnic bag before you leave for Britain and equip it for lunch on the go. When you arrive in London, purchase picnic lunch items from the elaborate food sections in the basement of Marks and Spencer, Harrods Food Hall, or a corner grocery. Assuming the weather is good, head for Hyde Park, Green Park, St. James's Park, Regent's Park … you get the idea.

Coleman makes an insulated bag with a shoulder strap; L.L. Bean has several packable coolers. Whatever you buy, equip it with a few things to make picnics easier:

- Swiss army knife (with clean blades)
- Disposable moist hand wipes
- Folded paper towels
- Plastic zip-top bags
- Lightweight, waterproof ground cloth
- Plastic knives, forks, spoons
- Corkscrew (for Mom and Dad's wine)

At the end of your trip, these padded insulated picnic bags are great for packing breakable souvenirs to carry home on the plane. With airport security restrictions, the knife and corkscrew obviously don't go in your airline carryon luggage.

Ready To Eat

In a country that invented the sandwich you would think that lunches would be a snap. There are a large number of sandwich shops throughout London and while these shops largely cater to business people on lunch breaks, they also work well for families in search of a quick lunch. *Pret a Manger* (literally "ready to eat") is a chain with fresh, reasonably priced lunchtime fare. Most patrons carry out food, but there are a limited number of tables in these sandwich shops. One advantage to carry out ("take away" in Britspeak) is that you do not have to pay the hefty Value Added Tax on cold food that you purchase.

Delis are a rarity in London, and late night food of any description can be hard to find in some sections of town. On one trip, after a long day of touring, we fed the children and put them to bed in our hotel room. But we parents were more hungry than tired, so I went out of the hotel to find a deli or sandwich shop. At 10:30 p.m. most of the stores in London's Mayfair section were long since closed. I jogged the back streets north of Piccadilly, passing numerous closed jewelers, art galleries and fashion boutiques. Finally I spotted a little sandwich shop with the lights still on. They were officially closed, but the Indian immigrant owner let me in. The shop had recently opened for business, and while he fixed me sandwiches, the owner peppered me with questions. "What about our prices? How much would you pay for a sandwich in America?" he inquired. "Well, it depends on where you are," I answered diplomatically. "In New York, the prices are about the same as yours, but in other areas things are less expensive." Next he wanted to know about the sodas I was buying. "Are they too expensive?" I stuck to diplomacy, had a nice conversation, and left with my expensive late night snack.

Tea Time

> 'At any rate I'll never go THERE again!' said Alice as she picked her way through the wood. 'It's the stupidest tea-party I ever was at in all my life!'
>
> —from *Alice's Adventures In Wonderland* by Lewis Carroll

Tea is not just a drink, it is a quintessential English dining and social experience. Tea comes in all varieties, costs, and degrees of formality. When traveling with children you've got a choice: find a less formal spot if your kids can't sit still for an hour, or if they're more patient, go whole hog and do afternoon tea.

Afternoon tea generally consists of tea (duh!), scones with jam and clotted cream, pastries or cake, and tea sandwiches. There is nothing low fat or low cholesterol about it. Will kids like it? Probably, and you can always order milk or something else to drink if they won't go for hot tea.

Sometimes tea can be substantial enough to serve as a substitute for dinner. Start the day with a full English breakfast, then eat a nutritious snack at lunchtime, followed up by tea late in the afternoon, and another snack before bed. This meal-snack-meal-snack routine is probably not recommended by nutritionists, but it has some advantages on a family trip to London. First, since finding kid-acceptable lunches and dinners can be problematic, substituting tea for dinner helps avoid the issue of where to eat a formal meal with children. Second, meal-snack-meal-snack fits well into a busy day of sightseeing because it provides several breaks where a family can sit down and revive with something to eat and drink before heading back to the tourist routes. Finally, breakfast and tea are relatively inexpensive meals that most children enjoy.

Teatime formality not withstanding, the staff at the restaurants in London's Fortnum and Mason department store seems to enjoy serving families. Well, maybe they just *tolerate* kids, but that's close enough. One afternoon, our children were restless after an hour's worth of tea, scones, and cake. A dutiful father, I got up from the table to let the kids wander in search of toys. Meanwhile the waitress implored my wife to stay and "relax away from the children … have another cuppa' and eat some more tarts!"

Many larger London hotels offer afternoon tea. Some—like the upscale Ritz, Four Seasons, and Brown's—are famous for over-the-top tea extravaganzas. But the average Londoner hardly has the time or the inclination for this level of tea ritual.

Pub Grub

So far we've covered breakfast, lunch, and tea. What about dinner? Some travel experts advise that British pub food is a good bet because it is cheap and filling. To be blunt, traditional London pub food can be pretty unappetizing to children. Try this on your kids: "Hey guys, let's order bangers and mash" (pork sausage served with mashed vegetables). Now *spotted dick* (don't ask), *that's* a true pub delicacy. Many London pubs serve vastly improved meals, with bangers and mash replaced by broiled fresh fish. But the upscale food can be accompanied by upscale prices and thereby negate the best feature of traditional pub fare.

In London, the pub scene is generally not geared toward families, but toward drinking beer and ale. In fact, some pubs do not even admit children. How can you tell whether a London pub is family-friendly? A few have signs posted near the door, but many do not, requiring mom or dad to walk in, find a pub employee, and ask before bringing in the kids. Yes, this can be intimidating.

Outside of London, pubs with family rooms are more common. The Four Alls pub in Welford-Upon-Avon is one example of a family-oriented pub. Welford is a few miles upstream from its heavily touristed neighbor Stratford-Upon-Avon. While staying a few days at a nearby farmhouse B&B, we toured the Cotswolds by day, wandering back to Welford each evening. Whether it was the decent food or the playground outside, the children kept suggesting that we return every night to the family room in "our" pub.

Family rooms in some pubs may also include pool tables and video games. Is this a good feature? You can draw your own conclusions.

Other Choices

As a city with many immigrants, London boasts a sizable number of ethnic restaurants; good news if your kids like Asian, Indian or Italian food. It is possible to find appetizing, reasonably priced meals in some of the city's ethnic establishments. It is also possible to find overpriced, uninspired food here.

With most children, you can't go wrong with pizza, but the trick in London is to find plain, American-style pizza. Cheese and tomato pizza sometimes features tomato slices instead of tomato sauce. This did not go over well with our kids, nor did the pizza with curry offered by a Pizza Hut in the Bayswater neighborhood. The Pizza Express chain is a popular London choice offering pizza, of course, along with other Italian dishes.

The Fountain Restaurant at Fortnum and Mason department store is also a good choice for dinner if you've got kids who can sit through a meal. The restaurant is only moderately expensive and it offers variety with some kid-friendly menu items. This is the kind of restaurant once found in American downtown department stores before they all moved to suburban shopping malls. When Fortnum and Mason is closed, enter the restaurant by a separate entrance at the rear of the store.

You can find informal, cafeteria-style food in some London churches, museums and historical sites. Here are just a few examples:

- St. Martin-in-the-Fields Crypt Café (see Brass Rubbing section).
- Institute of Contemporary Arts ICAfé near the Mall (you must pay the museum admission fee to get in, even just to eat at the café).
- A cafeteria in the basement of Central Hall Westminster, right across the street from Westminster Abbey.
- The Armouries cafeteria on the grounds of the Tower of London.

Wagamama, the ubiquitous noodle chain, offers inexpensive and fresh Asian-inspired noodle dishes in locations throughout London. Wagamamas are usually clean and spartan, but for kids who enjoy noodle-based soups and other dishes, this is a good choice. Coffee shops are everywhere in central London, with Starbucks trying its best to flood the city, but there are other choices, like Café Nero, which offer more food choices than the Seattle mega-chain.

Be aware that many traditional British restaurants do not open for dinner until 7:00 or 7:30 p.m. Tired young children (and their parents) may starve by then! Fortunately London has sprouted a number of moderately priced chain restaurants which serve dinner earlier. In this case, the term "chain restaurant" does not mean fast food places like McDonald's or Burger King, although you'll find these in London too. We're referring to real sit-down restaurants like Bella Pasta, Café Rouge, Dôme, Café Uno, Francofill, and Rôtisserie Jules, to name a few. These places are informal, reasonable (by London standards) and, best of all, you don't have to wait until 7:30 p.m. to feed the family. Our visit to Bella Pasta just off Oxford Street featured a family-pleasing menu—logically weighted toward pasta—with a friendly, genuine Italian staff. To make the meal even more of a bargain, look in tourist publications for discount coupons that can be used at some of these restaurant chains.

Plan ahead since the areas surrounding some popular tourist spots like St. Paul's Cathedral and the Tower of London don't have many family dining options. To be honest, there is often a McDonald's within walking distance of many of London's greatest historical sights. Talk about a contrast between history and modern culture!

And if you want to take the family out for a special meal? London has hundreds of moderate-to-expensive restaurants; many independent, some allied in upscale restaurant chains. For example, Conran Restaurants, founded by designer Terrance Conran, operates an eclectic group of restaurants around the city. Some of these, like the Bluebird restaurant complex in trendy Chelsea, are popular with families. Keep in mind that restaurant meals in London are much more expensive than in most American cities.

Special Treats

A visit to London may broaden your children's food horizons. After discovering it in England, our son now craves Nutella sandwiches.

Nutella is a chocolate hazelnut spread, sort of a peanut butter for chocoholics. Our son also targeted the ever-present Cadbury vending machines which dispensed the best chocolate bars he had ever tasted. His notes on the subject follow, and we defer to him as an expert:

- The machines in train and Tube stations are usually out of plain milk chocolate bars. They've always got the bars with nuts or raisins!
- Use exact change in Cadbury vending machines since some machines reject larger amounts.
- Convince your parents to buy lots of Cadbury bars at the tax free shops in the airport before you come home—they need to use up all that leftover British money before the plane takes off.
- The Cadbury bars sold in the United States don't taste as good as the ones in the United Kingdom.

Our compliments and apologies to the Cadbury chocolate empire.

Our daughter, who is older and had a more adventurous palate, discovered her affinity for scones topped with jam and clotted cream. On another trip she started drinking hot tea. Since one can survive on English breakfasts and afternoon tea, this basically ended the food crisis from her perspective.

Fish and chips is another traditional English favorite that goes over fairly well with many children. The dwindling number of London "chippies" offer a variety of fish, but a mild white fish like cod may be the best choice for kids. The fish is fried, as are the chips of course, but you tend to walk off a lot of fattening food while touring London. Finally, kids in search of plain food can always order a "jacket" (baked potato) in almost any food establishment.

PART 5

Did You Forget Anything?

Passport? Check! Suitcase? Check! Bermuda Shorts?

Passports

U.S. and Canadian citizens need a valid passport to enter Britain. That includes the whole family and children of all ages must have their own passports. Most post offices and many county courts process passport applications. In addition to a completed application form, you need the following items to get a U.S. passport:

- A certified birth certificate or expired passport as proof of age and citizenship.
- Current photo identification, such as a driver's license or government ID card.
- Two identical passport sized photographs.
- Money—passport fees are hefty, but at least the passport is valid for 10 years.
- Patience.

We mention the last item because it can take four to eight weeks to receive a passport by mail. Need a passport in a hurry? There are commercial services that offer fast turnaround for a price and for an added fee the U.S. State Department will expedite passport processing.

As we noted, children must have a passport to travel internationally and the U.S. passport application process generally requires the participation of both parents to apply for a child's passport. Even with a valid passport, there are strict requirements for international travel by children when they are not accompanied by both parents. The protections are in place to guard against incidents where one parent flees the country with a child in a custody dispute. Travel restrictions can come as a surprise, where custody is not at issue, when one parent (or a grandparent) tries to go on an overseas vacation with a child. Generally, a notarized letter with specific consent for travel, signed by both parents, is advisable.

For more on the U.S. passport process, including updates on new passport features and requirements, check the State Department's website at http://travel.state.gov.

Luggage

> From the carpet-bag she took out seven flannel nightgowns, four cotton ones, a pair of boots, a set of dominoes, two bathing-caps and a postcard album. Last of all came a folding camp-bedstead with blankets and eiderdown complete, and this she set down between John's cot and Barbara's.
>
> —from *Mary Poppins* by P. L. Travers

Advice on packing is *de rigueur* for most self-respecting travel guidebooks. Guess that means we have to include a section on the subject, but we preface it with a confession: we enjoy planning and taking trips; we hate packing and transporting luggage. Short trips of a week or less are not too bad, but packing two or three weeks worth of clothing and accessories for a family trip is a challenge.

Since the weather can vary so greatly, there is no ideal way to pack for a trip to London. Even in the summer months we suggest planning a layered wardrobe: short sleeve shirts, over which you can put a sweater and add a water-repellent jacket with a hood or hat. Dark colors don't show much dirt and, with a little luck, children can wear a pair of dark pants for more than one day. If possible, pack clothes in colors and styles that can be mixed and matched easily.

It is virtually impossible to carry enough clean clothes for more than eight or nine days, especially when traveling with kids. On longer trips, this means doing laundry (Arghh!). Hotel laundry services are very expensive, but you can find launderettes in some central London neighborhoods. Spending time in a laundromat is not our idea of vacation fun. We've done it on long trips, but it does seem like a waste of valuable touring time.

Since children often manage to get spots and stains on otherwise clean clothes, pack some disposable stain removal wipes for quick cleanups. Also, take along some large zip-top plastic bags to store shoes and dirty clothes. These sound like *Hints From Heloise*, don't they?

The more you pack, the heavier the luggage becomes, and not every child can lift a heavy suitcase. We suggest using relatively inexpensive, but sturdy, wheeled suitcases with good wide rollers and telescoping handles that allow you to easily roll the bags. Test luggage before you buy since some suitcases tend to tip over easily and tippy luggage is no fun when you are running to catch a train or an elevator.

Even with wheels, there are times when you will have to lift your suitcases, so make sure you can manage your bags. While some children may not be able to pick up a big suitcase, most kids are quite adept at carrying a heavy backpack to school every day. So consider backpacks or daypacks as part of the family luggage compliment. Small backpacks also work well as airplane carry-ons and can be used for picnics and hiking excursions during a trip. And while we are on the subject of airplanes and luggage, airline baggage allowances and restrictions are a major consideration when packing for your trip. The allowances vary by cabin, with first and business class passengers permitted to check more luggage than coach class passengers.

Finally, buy some cloth ribbon in two bright colors and tie a piece of each color on all your bags and backpacks. Busy airports are filled with look-alike bags, and many people go to the trouble to mark their baggage. But it is unlikely that anyone else will pick the same two colors of ribbon as you did, tie them on suitcases that look just like yours, and get on the same airplane. The ribbon helps you spot your suitcases at the airport baggage claim carousel, and when you check into a hotel it is simple to just tell the bellperson to grab everything with the orange and purple ribbons. We also like cheeky luggage tags that read *This is NOT your bag*, but if they catch on and everyone uses them, what good will they be?

In case you haven't heard, it can rain in Britain. A lot. Before your trip, consider purchasing several cans of waterproof fabric spray and spraying everything: your shoes, jackets and coats, hats, backpacks, the children. On second thought, don't waterproof the kids, but do spray just about everything else. This will really come in handy if it rains. Plus, if you go to all this effort it probably won't rain one drop.

Blending In

You may be a tourist in London, but you don't have to look like one. Londoners sport all varieties of fashion, but few of them dress like stereotypical American tourists. You know the outfit: cameras, plaid Bermuda shorts, white tennis shoes, T-shirts and *gimme caps*. Beyond dressing like a tourist, some visitors just act like tourists. Unfolding and studying large maps while standing in the middle of a crowded sidewalk is a sure sign of a tourist. If you want to blend in, dress conservatively and tastefully, carry a small camera in a pocket or bag, buy a compact fold-out map and study it before you hit the street. Dressing conservatively and tastefully does not necessarily mean dressing up. Casual clothes are usually fine in London, but dark slacks and decent shirts blend in better than sweatsuits and T-shirts advertising your favorite brand of beer.

Cultural stereotypes are problematic, but one other characteristic often associated with American tourists is loudness. Visitors who want to blend in should take this into consideration. Failure to use correct British terminology is another blend in faux pas. Asking for directions to "the bathroom" instead of using the British terms *loo, gents, or ladies* marks you as a sure tourist. On the other hand, don't go overboard and adopt a fake British accent—Londoners will know you are not a native anyway.

Camera? Check! Travel Journal? Check! Tape Recorder?

Cameras

Inexpensive digital cameras, or cheap disposable cameras, are great vacation ideas for kids. Secretly pack a couple of these then distribute them to the children after you arrive in London, maybe when things get a little slow or the kids get bored. Digital cameras have the advantage of instant gratification—what you shoot, you see right away. Disposable cameras aren't just kid stuff either; adults can take along a disposable panoramic camera to get all of Trafalgar Square or Buckingham Palace into one shot! You won't get Ansell Adams' quality, but inexpensive digital cameras and disposable cameras work surprisingly well.

With digital cameras, be sure to have a large enough media card to hold lots of shots. The cards that come standard with many digital cameras are usually inadequate. Although you can download images from the camera to a computer, this either means carrying a laptop or using a download service while in London.

Film in England is very expensive, so consider bringing along a supply from home if you are using a film camera. Remove film canisters from their boxes and pack the film in a clear plastic bag. To avoid damage to film when you go through airport security checks, ask to have the film and camera hand-inspected rather than x-rayed. Depending upon the security climate, the inspectors may oblige. During periods of increased airport security, cameras may not be allowed in carryon luggage. Do not pack film in your checked luggage since the x-rays used to inspect airplane cargo are more powerful and will damage film. Some experts suggest buying a lead foil lined film bag, but if the bag shows up as a solid object in the x-rays of your luggage, the security operator may just crank up the juice on the x-ray machine and *really* fry your film. If you want to limit x-ray damage, consider developing film before returning home. There are a number of one-hour photo developers in central London.

Before leaving on the trip, replace all camera batteries. If your camera has not been used recently, test it thoroughly before you leave to make sure the camera is working properly. Finding out that your camera was malfunctioning is one surprise you don't want when you get home from your trip.

If you take a video camera, or a rechargeable digital still camera, make sure you have some way of charging the batteries in Britain where the electric current is 220 volts versus the 110 volt American standard. Many cameras operate on dual currents, but make certain before plugging yours in. You'll also need a plug adaptor because electrical plugs in Britain differ from those in the United States and Canada.

Computers

Taking a laptop computer on your trip is a mixed blessing. Many travelers want or need to check email to keep in touch online during vacations. But for the traveler, laptops and other electrical devices engender additional security screening at airports. Then there's the weight and bulk of packing and carrying even the smallest laptop on your trip, along with concerns about loss or theft. Quality London hotels usually offer in-room high-speed and/or wireless internet access, but they often charge exorbitant fees for getting online. Most modern laptops operate on dual currents—both 110 volts (North America) and

220 volts (Europe). You will need a plug adaptor to connect your laptop to those distinctive British electrical outlets.

There are internet cafés in London, where you can get online for a couple of pounds. This can be a cheaper option than paying hotel connection charges, although public computers (and clientele) can be a bit grubby at some locations. There are also numerous wireless hotspots in London, some of which offer free service.

Postcards, Scrapbooks And Journals

As a family activity, mail yourselves a postcard from London. Buy a postcard showing your favorite London site and write a note to yourselves about what a wonderful trip you are having. Then find a mail box—only an old fashioned red British post box will do—and take a photograph of your children as they mail the postcard home. When you get back from vacation, the postcard and the photo are great additions to a child's scrapbook.

A trip to Britain gives kids ample opportunity to collect things: ticket stubs from trains, theaters, museums, and other spots; brochures and handouts from hotels, airplanes and tourist information counters. If you rent a car and tour the countryside, your children may want to collect the dozens of *pay and display* parking lot stubs that will accumulate on the windshield and dashboard. Consider relaxing your parental invective to throw away all this junk. Letting the children collect ticket stubs, brochures, and pay and display tickets serves as a record of your trip. Intersperse this collected material with photographs and you'll have the makings of a family scrapbook.

Another way to record the trip is to take along travel diaries for every family member. Most school-age children can use the practice with their writing skills and young artists may even want to include drawings in their diaries. At the end of each day on the trip, take a few minutes to write in the diaries. After a busy day of touring, it may be all you can do to stay awake long enough to fill a page. But it is surprising how fast the details of a vacation can be forgotten, so a diary can be an important way to help preserve travel memories.

Sights And Sounds

Sight*seeing* is on every tourist's agenda, but to fully appreciate London be prepared to *listen* as you tour the city. Some examples:

- Be anywhere within 500 feet of Big Ben at noon.
- Listen for accents. The trained ear will hear a variety of accented English—some typically British, some not. Watch out or you're liable to start speaking with a British "twist" after a few days.
- Listen to the organist practice in Westminster Abbey or stop by a lunchtime concert at St. Martin-in-the-Fields church.

On one visit, our children wished they had brought a tape or digital recorder just to capture the different sounds—train whistles, church bells, station announcements in the Tube, overheard conversations of British children, shouted commands at the changing of the guards—all uniquely British and all a part of their trip memories.

Guardians Of The Past

Visitors to Britain will find that many historic sights are owned or operated by one of two organizations: The National Trust or English Heritage. The Trust is a non-profit group that preserves historic land, gardens and buildings in Britain. English Heritage is very similar except that it is government-backed. Each organization operates a different set of properties, but there is some overlap. At Stonehenge for example, the National Trust owns the land and English Heritage operates the site.

A visitor's pass from one of these organizations can save on admission to historic sights, however, neither organization operates many of the major tourist sights in London. Visitors who are not venturing out of the city may not save enough to justify purchasing a pass.

In addition to separate passes from the National Trust and English Heritage, VisitBritain, the British tourism agency, sells a combination pass that may be right for you. Families traveling to Britain need to evaluate the merits of purchasing passes based on their itineraries and the ages of their children. Most passes are sold in adult and child versions, but many of the historic sites already offer reduced admission prices for children. On one trip we found that purchasing passes for the two adults and paying cash for the children's admission tickets made the most economic sense.

Keep in mind that many major museums in London offer free admission, so don't buy a pass assuming that you will save money on museum tickets.

The Great British Heritage Pass

This pass provides free entry into many properties belonging to the National Trust and English Heritage. The pass also gets you into some important privately owned properties like Blenheim Palace. The list of properties is impressive, but the pass covers relatively few places in London. Heritage Passes can be purchased for 4, 7, 15 or 30 days. You can buy the pass online from the British tourism agency at www.visitbritain.com.

English Heritage Overseas Visitor Pass

This pass gets you into English Heritage sites only. It covers 7 or 14 days. English Heritage properties in London include the Chapter House in Westminster Abbey, the Jewel Tower near Parliament, Kenwood House, and the Wellington Arch. You can purchase the pass online at www.english-heritage.org.uk or at many English Heritage operated properties in Britain. English Heritage also offers annual memberships that include admission to sites.

National Trust And Royal Oak

The National Trust sells passes of different lengths that provide entry into Trust properties. Americans can also join the Royal Oak Foundation, an affiliate of the Trust, and get free admission to all Trust properties for a year. A family Royal Oak membership is a relative bargain. Like English Heritage, the National Trust operates only a few properties in central London. Information on properties, passes, and memberships can be found on the National Trust website at www.nationaltrust.org.uk and the Royal Oak website at www.royal-oak.org.

Historic Royal Palaces Pass

Historic Royal Palaces is the governmental agency that administers Hampton Court Palace, Kensington Palace, the Banqueting House, Tower of London, Kew Palace, and Queen Charlotte's Cottage. The agency sells passes that admit visitors to several palaces at a cost savings over individual admission charges. You can purchase passes and individual tickets online at www.hrp.org.uk. Historic Royal Palaces offers annual memberships as well.

London Pass

The London Pass is a widely promoted commercial pass that provides admission to many tourist attractions in London. The London Pass is expensive, so you'll need to look over the list of attractions covered before you purchase one of these cards to make certain you will get your money's worth. In general, to make the card worthwhile, you need to visit a fair number of sights that charge admission fees during a relatively short period. One side benefit of the London Pass is that passholders usually get to bypass regular ticket lines. The London Pass website is www.londonpass.com.

Getting There—Look! It's A Bird, It's An Eight Hour Plane Ride

Most airlines favor overnight flights to Britain, leaving the American East Coast in the evenings and arriving somewhere between 7:00 a.m. and 10:00 a.m. London time the next day. While it does mean one less night you have to spend in a hotel, the overnight trip is a drag on the whole family. Return flights are somewhat easier because they usually leave in the early afternoon and, flying with the sun, you arrive in the East Coast around dinnertime. You still spend at least seven hours in the air though.

There are some East Coast flights which leave in the morning and arrive in London the same evening (local times). An advantage of this schedule is that it avoids an overnight flight and may reduce the effects of jet lag.

Travelers coming from the central U.S. have similar flight choices, although the total travel time is longer than for East Coast departures. West Coast travelers face nearly ten hours in the air on a direct flight to London. Direct flights leaving Los Angeles at 6:00 p.m. arrive in London around noon the next day. This is a long flight and some families may prefer to break it up with an overnight stop on the East Coast.

This section examines plane trip survival tips for families on the flight segment from the U.S. East Coast to London and back. These tips can be adjusted for longer flights.

If you leave the East Coast on an evening flight around 7:00 p.m., consider eating dinner a short while before you get on board. Once airborne, refuse the meal on the plane. This may earn you some funny looks from the flight attendants, but if you eat a big dinner on the plane at 8:00 or 9:00 p.m. Eastern Standard Time, you'll still be offered breakfast only four hours later as the plane approaches the United Kingdom. This out-of-sync meal schedule can add to jet lag.

The trick on the flight to Britain is to adjust to a London schedule as soon as you can, so set your watch to London time when you get on the plane. Wow, it's midnight already, time to go to sleep! Now convince your kids (and yourself) that the next seven hours on the plane are actually a normal night: you ate dinner at 6:00 p.m., got on the plane at 7:00 p.m., went to bed early at 8:00 p.m., tried to sleep for 5 hours, woke up and had breakfast, then the plane landed in London. Okay, it's really 2:00 a.m. Eastern Standard Time when you arrive in London and you probably got no real sleep on the plane, but you have to believe it was a normal night or you'll fall asleep just as you get into London. This schedule almost works, especially if it is a bright, sunny morning when you get off the plane since sunlight seems to reduce the impact of jet lag.

The best way to see this is with a time line:

What time is it at home?	in London?	What you are trying to do	What's going on in the plane
6:00 p.m. EST	11:00 p.m.	Finish a light dinner and get ready to board.	Pre-boarding announcements and endless waiting.
7:00 p.m.	midnight	Settle in. Complain about how cramped economy class is. Drink some water. Hit the restroom.	Takeoff and welcome aboard!
8:00 p.m.	1:00 a.m.	Sleep! (or at least some serious resting).	Drinks anyone? Dinner is served (eventually).

9:00 p.m.	2:00 a.m.	Sleep!	More drinks? Let's start that movie!
10:00 p.m.	3:00 a.m.	Sleep!	Movie ... duty-free shopping?
11:00 p.m.	4:00 a.m.	Sleep!	Lights out! Time for your 90 minute beauty rest. Of course the people in the seats behind you keep talking loudly.
midnight	5:00 a.m.	Wake up, visit the restroom before the line forms.	Wake up! Line up for the restrooms. Breakfast is served.
1:00 a.m.	6:00 a.m.	Eat breakfast. Get a coffee refill.	Last chance to buy duty free goods. Customs forms and welcome video.
2:00 a.m.	7:00 a.m.	Take off on your London adventure in reasonably good shape.	Thank you for flying with us. Try not to fall asleep before clearing customs.

Once you land in London, try to follow a normal schedule. You'll be tired, but don't take a nap (unless afternoon naps are still a part of your child's daily routine). If caffeine helps you, grab some coffee or tea early in the day. Eat meals at regular London times and stay awake until at least 9:00 p.m. In theory, by the next day you should have made the switch to London time. Good luck with this routine, particularly if you are traveling with young children.

Flying business or first class across the Atlantic can be a better experience. Upper class seats usually convert to flat "beds" making it relatively easy to get a few hours of real sleep on the journey. Business class passengers can even get showers, spa treatments, and breakfast at special arrivals lounges in London airports. Ahhh....

For families, the airplane trip to Britain is trying, at best. We've outlined a possible schedule to ease the transition, but what else can you do to make your children more comfortable on the flight?

Motion Sickness And Ear Problems

If your child is prone to motion sickness be prepared before you step foot on the plane. Check with a pediatrician about whether your child can safely take motion sickness medication. Drowsiness is one side effect of some medications and that's not a bad thing if you are trying to sleep on the plane, but dehydration is another possible side effect. Drinking lots of water can have other unwanted side effects for children, especially considering the lines for restrooms on crowded airplanes. But since the cabin air is very dry, do stay hydrated.

Our children have had some success with another motion sickness remedy—pressure point wristbands sold under the brand name Sea-Band. These elastic bands apply gentle pressure to a point on the inside of each wrist. How and why they work is a mystery to us. Is it a scientific principle or is it like the "magic feather" that convinced Dumbo the Elephant that he could fly? Regardless of how they work, wristbands may be a drug-free alternative for preventing motion sickness.

If you expect motion sickness to be a problem, be prepared for the worst. Pack a change of clothes in a zip-top plastic bag so if the child gets sick, you'll have clean clothes and a place to stash any dirty garments. If motion sickness is inevitable for your child, consider dressing him or her in an old sweatsuit, then throw it away if it gets messed up. Wasteful, yes, but do you really want to carry a plastic bag with barfed-on clothes until you get to your hotel in London? To paraphrase Thomas Paine: "These are the times that try parents' souls."

Another motion sickness suggestion is to feed children only small amounts of bland food before and during the flight. This may help prevent sickness and, if not, you'll still be grateful you followed this advice.

Our son had a well-deserved reputation as a picky eater and he had a tendency to get motion sick. After flights to and from London at ages six, eight, and ten, he began to associate the very smell of airline food with airsickness. His solution: eat *nothing* on the plane. That was a bit extreme and he eventually conceded the need to stash a bland snack in his carry-on baggage.

Changes in air pressure can cause ear problems for children and adults on an airplane. You can try giving children something to chew during takeoff and landing and babies can suck the heck out their pacifiers to equalize pressure. There are also earplugs available that use ceramic filters to slowly equalize air pressure. The disposable earplugs (brand name EarPlanes) are designed to work for only two flight segments and are made in sizes for children ages 3 to 11 and adults (anyone over 12). The earplugs also block out some noise, so they have an added benefit if you are trying to sleep on the plane.

Seating Arrangements

Airplane seating has become a not-so-funny joke as hundreds of passengers are crammed into narrow seats with almost no leg room. If your family is lucky enough to travel first or business class, sit back, relax and enjoy the flight. Otherwise, read on for some survival tips.

Adults can usually survive a restless airborne night, but young children often fall apart without sleep. If the airplane is not crowded, you may be able to let your children stretch out across several seats (but still with a seat belt fastened). However, during peak travel times when most families are on the go, planes tend to be packed. Two adults traveling with one or two children may want to get window seats for the kids, with one adult in the seat next to each child. This works well on planes with rows of two seats by the cabin wall: parent and child can travel side-by-side with no strangers sitting next to them. When it is time to sleep, the kids can at least prop a pillow against the cabin wall or lean against Mom or Dad.

Seats just in front of a bulkhead are good because there will be no noisy people behind you when you are trying to sleep. Keep in mind that the seats just in front of a bulkhead may not recline as much as other seats. Some parents prefer seats facing a bulkhead and at one time airlines suggested this location because children could play on the floor here. We strongly recommend that children and adults wear seat belts throughout the flight, so playing on the floor is not an option, but seating near a bulkhead does provide a sense of extra privacy. Some airlines offer special seats/cots for children under age two. The seats attach to a cabin bulkhead wall and allow the child to lie down or sit up. If you want to arrange for this, check with your airline when you make reservations. Anyone who does not have a young child may want to avoid bulkhead seats.

Although airlines do allow an infant to be held in the lap of an adult, we question the safety of this practice and the sanity anyone who plans to hold a baby for the duration of an overseas plane ride. The "lap baby" fare is cheap, but buying a separate seat for a baby allows parents to use an approved child safety seat or harness onboard. Seats or harnesses must be approved for use on an airplane by the U.S. Federal Aviation Administration and/or the British Civil Aviation Authority.

Generally, seats over the wings near the center of the plane have a smoother ride than seating near the tail or the nose. Think of a plane as a seesaw—the least motion will be near the center pivot point rather than the ends. Note to nervous flyers: *don't* think of an airplane as a seesaw, think of it as a puffy cloud gliding calmly through a bright blue sky.

Some airlines have eliminated the practice of allowing passengers to pre-select seating locations. If you join the airline's frequent flier program you may find it easier to pre-select your seats. Regardless of the airline's stated policy, decide in advance where you want to sit. Let the airline know you are traveling with children and request your preferred seat assignment when you purchase your tickets and again when you check-in for the flight. At the gate, families with young children can sometimes board first. Listen for the boarding announcement to take advantage of this privilege.

The Class System

Most families fly coach/economy class out of economic necessity. If you are fortunate enough to fly business class or—*thank you Lord!*— first class, your flight to Britain can be a totally different experience. The flight times are the same, although someone once pointed out that passengers in the front of the airplane arrive a fraction of a second ahead of coach passengers seated in the back. But the business class experience from boarding to landing can be much less stressful, with faster check-in, larger baggage allowances, separate departure and arrival lounges, better food, and humanely sized seating. On British Airways and Virgin Atlantic flat bed business class service, passengers can actually get real sleep on the way to London. Virgin Atlantic even calls this "upper class" as if we need reminding that the class system operates in the air. Business class is always an improvement, even without flat bed seats. Newer, all business class airlines also serve the U.S. to U.K. market.

Recognizing that not everyone can afford to fly business class, airlines have added so-called "premium economy" service. For a moderate increase in ticket price, this class adds more legroom and a slight upgrade in amenities and service. Premium economy can be a good compromise for traveling families.

If you have a moderate balance of frequent flier points, paying for a lower class seat and using miles to upgrade is another way to improve the flight experience without going broke.

In-Flight Distractions

Sleep is the goal of veteran airline travelers crossing the Atlantic. Some go so far as to make *Do Not Disturb* signs out of self-adhesive mailing labels and stick them on their seat headrests. Despite looking dorky, this cuts down on late night interruptions by the cabin crew:

Them: Will you be drinking red or white wine with our fabulous dinner?

You: Snork. Huh? Do you have Juicy Juice?

Them: Would you like to buy duty free goods?

You: It's 3:00 a.m. No thanks!

On the flight to London, wise travelers are trying to sleep or rest, and avoiding in-flight distractions is one strategy. It is easy for adults to ignore the in-flight movies and video entertainment, but it may be a challenge to keep your children from watching movies or playing with the seatback video displays.

If sleep is impossible on the plane, you face at least six and a half hours of entertaining your restless children. Fortunately, on long overseas flights most airlines provide activity kits for kids. These are good for an hour or so ... then what? Listening to the audio channels or watching the in-flight movies and games? Airline entertainment is usually pretty mild—movies rated PG, PG-13, or edited to remove the most objectionable stuff—but it may still not be appropriate for your children. For alternative entertainment let each child carry a small backpack filled with paperback books, small games or toys, journal/sketchbook, markers and pens, maybe even a stuffed animal. Don't pack expensive items that may get lost on a long trip.

A special note about Fluffy the Bear (or whatever your child's favorite stuffed animal is named). If Fluffy absolutely must go on the trip, plan in advance how to keep track of him. Perhaps Fluffy needs his own identifying luggage tag. Maybe he really would like to "ride" in the suitcase or backpack and only come out at bedtime. Tracking down Fluffy if he gets left in an airport lounge, on the plane, in a taxi, on a train, or in a hotel is not how you want to spend your travel time and emotional energy!

London's Airports

Most flights from North America arrive at one of two London airports: Heathrow, about 16 miles west of central London; or Gatwick, 28 miles due south of downtown. A few flights from U.S. also arrive at London's Stansted Airport, which is over 40 miles north of central London.

Generally speaking, arriving at Gatwick is less complicated because it is smaller and not as busy as Heathrow. Getting to downtown London is easy because there is frequent, fast train service from the airport to Victoria station—the trip takes 30-40 minutes. If you are not heading for downtown London, or if Victoria station is not convenient, you can take trains from the Gatwick rail station to other locations around London. The non-express trains take a few minutes longer, but cost less. Because it is 28 miles away, taking a taxi from Gatwick to central London is an expensive and lengthy proposition.

Thanks to Gatwick's layout, which includes an elevated shuttle train between terminals, you can use a luggage cart almost all the way from baggage pick-up at the airport to the taxi stand at London's Victoria station. Victoria is convenient for hotels and attractions near Buckingham Palace and south of Hyde Park.

Arriving at Heathrow? The size of this airport can be daunting, as are the transportation choices. Heathrow has its own high-speed rail link from the airport to Paddington train station in downtown London. Travel time is about 20 minutes. There is a non-express train that follows this same route too. Paddington is very convenient for hotels in Bloomsbury, Mayfair, and areas north of Hyde Park. There are also London Underground stops at Heathrow, although anyone with children and/or much luggage probably should avoid the Tube at this point in their journey. Finally, a taxi ride from Heathrow to downtown is certainly possible, albeit expensive. During rush hours, the Tube and taxi options are more challenging.

The Stansted Express is the fastest connection to that remote London airport. The train runs frequently and takes about 45 minutes to reach London's Liverpool Street rail station.

The National Express company also operates various bus and bus/rail connections to London's airports that may be convenient if you are staying in certain locations in the city or connecting from other locations in Britain. One popular route circles between the airport and major downtown hotels.

Finally, booking an airport transfer service can be a logistically simple way to get between London and its airports. Reliable services meet visitors at the airport and take them directly to their hotels. Transfer services tend to be a bit less expensive than genuine London taxis, but they are less strictly regulated, so service levels and prices can vary. However, with London's heavy traffic, it is hard for any on-the-road transportation service to beat the express rail services.

Green Travel

Flying on an airplane contributes to global warming by spewing carbon dioxide and other pollutants into the atmosphere. Leisure travelers face an ethical dilemma since their trips are by choice rather than necessity. As awareness grows, some airlines are adopting carbon neutral policies and including environmental fees within ticket prices and some governments are imposing environmental fees on tickets. One way individuals can offset the impact of travel is to purchase carbon credits through an environmental organization. Some resources include the Carbon Fund (www.carbonfund.org) and Climate Crisis (www.climatecrisis.net).

*   *   *

Where? When? £?

British Airports Authority (Gatwick and Heathrow Information)

Website   www.baa.co.uk

Heathrow Express (rail)

Website   www.heathrowexpress.com

Heathrow Connect (rail)

Website   www.heathrowconnect.com

Gatwick Express (rail)

Website   www.gatwickexpress.com

Stansted Express (rail)

Website   www.stanstedexpress.com

National Express (bus)

Website   www.nationalexpress.com

Getting Around Town

Which is the way to London Town,
To see the King in his golden crown?
One foot up and one foot down,
That's the way to London Town.

Which is the way to London Town,
To see the Queen in her silken gown?
Left! Right! Left! Right! up and down,
Soon you'll be in London Town!

Which is the way to London Town?
Over the hills, across the down;
Over the ridges and over the bridges,
That is the way to London Town.

And what shall I see in London Town?
Many a building old and brown.
Many a real, old-fashioned street
You'll be sure to see in London Town.

—Traditional children's rhyme

Finding Your Way

In London, the term *street plan* is an oxymoron. There is no plan to London's streets. This city has evolved from the plans laid down in Roman times. It was abandoned, burned, then rebuilt by Saxons, Normans and Victorian reformers. Finally, London was flattened by

Nazi bombs, rebuilt and modernized. The result? Tourists need a good map and a fair sense of direction to avoid becoming hopelessly lost.

Even without a map, there are clues to finding your way in London. No, we don't mean relying on the position of the sun to determine east and west. We have tried this method, but it is useless at night or in cloudy weather, something London has an abundance of. Instead we suggest you become familiar with London's postal codes. They have a certain logic to them. For example *N* means north and *W* is west. The postal code gives an indication of your location relative to central London. Unfortunately, the numbers that make up the rest of the postal code are no help to the lost tourist and sometimes they appear to have been assigned at random. If you are in zone W1, don't count on finding zone W2 around the next corner.

Some sample postal codes:

Codes	The Neighborhood	Important Sights
W1	Mayfair, Marylebone	Royal Academy of Arts, shopping along Oxford, Regents and Piccadilly streets
W2	Paddington, Bayswater	Hyde Park, Little Venice
WC1	Bloomsbury	British Museum
WC2	Strand, Covent Garden	London Transport Museum, National Gallery, Trafalgar Square
W8	Kensington	Kensington Palace
SW7	Knightsbridge, South Kensington	Victoria and Albert Museum, Science Museum, Natural History Museum
SW1	Westminster	Parliament, Westminster Abbey, Buckingham Palace, Victoria rail station, Downing Street, Cabinet War Rooms

EC3	City of London (east)	Tower of London
EC4	City of London	St. Paul's Cathedral
NW1	Regent's Park, Marylebone	Zoo, Sherlock Holmes Museum, Regent's Park
SE1	Southwark	Globe Theatre, HMS Belfast, Imperial War Museum, Tower Bridge

When planning a trip to London, intrepid internet explorers can use online mapping websites to help locate streets in the city. Simply enter a street name or postal code and the website provides color maps of the area at various levels of detail. Watch out for outdated maps, even on the internet. For use in London, most visitors will want to choose a map of the city, balancing portability against level of detail. Tiny, foldable pocket maps are easy to carry and inconspicuous; maps with more details can be huge and ungainly.

If London seems large, it's because it *is* large. Trivia fans and lost tourists will want to know that London is about 580 square miles big, and filled with about seven million residents.

Subway And Bus

> Paddington decided the Underground was quite the most exciting thing that had ever happened to him ... "I shall always travel on this Underground in the future," said Paddington, politely. "I'm sure it's the nicest in all London."
>
> —from *A Bear Called Paddington* by Michael Bond

Thank heavens for London's Underground (Tube) and bus system, because driving in London would be a tourist's worst nightmare. By all means use the Tube and bus as your primary means of transport in the city.

Kids generally enjoy trips on both the Tube and London's famous red double-decker buses (riding on the top level in the front seats, of course). A word of caution however—avoid rush hours! The crush on the Tube is disconcerting for a six-foot tall adult; it can be frightening for a four-foot tall child. On the surface, bus travel during rush hour is maddeningly slow. It is often faster to walk than take the bus in central London during peak travel times. Anything before 9:30 a.m. on weekdays is considered peak hours—with more crowding and higher Tube fares. Hours to avoid are generally weekdays from 8:00 a.m. to 9:30 a.m. and 4:30 p.m. to 6:00 p.m. Approximate operating hours for the Tube are:

- Monday—Thursday from about 5:00 a.m. to just after midnight
- Friday—5:00 a.m. until 1:00 a.m. (Saturday morning)
- Saturday—7:00 a.m. until 1:00 a.m. (Sunday morning)
- Sunday–7:30 a.m. to 12:00 p.m.

Don't cut it too close since the times of the last trains vary by station. Transport for London divides the city into travel *zones* and most of the central London tourist attractions are located in Zone 1. Further afield, suburban Kew Gardens is in Zone 4. So you will want to choose your ticket option based on when you will travel, where you'll go and how long you are staying.

Transport for London offers a very confusing array of ticket options. There are individual trip tickets, single and multi-day *travelcards*, and electronic *Oyster* cards. Cash purchase of single tickets is the most expensive way to go—almost three times as costly as fares on the electronic cards.

Paper travelcards make sense for many visitors. The cards are good on buses, the Underground/Tube, local train travel, and the Docklands Light Railway. You can purchase one, three, or seven day peak and off-peak travelcards for a variety of zone combinations. Travelcards can be purchased online and mailed to you in advance of your trip. Try to match the number of days of the Travelcard to the length of your visit. Decide if you'll actually use it on your days of arrival and departure. The clock starts running the first time you use the Travelcard.

The electronic Oyster card is very convenient for London residents; less so for tourists. But the fares for Oyster users are generally the lowest, in fact, there is a daily price cap on the cards, no matter how far or often you travel. Actually, it's more complicated than that, but the price cap is still worthwhile. Oyster cards can be purchased online or in London from Tube stations and other locations. You pay a deposit for the card, then load it with money, again choosing from a variety of options. Simple it is not!

Transport for London's confusing fare options get even more confusing for families who want to take advantage of reduced fares for children. Children under age ten travel free and do not need tickets, Travelcards, or Oystercards when accompanied by an adult. Children ages 11 to 15 travel for very low cost, but may need a photo ID issued by Transport for London, which is hardly practical for most overseas visitors.

So what's the best deal? If you are bargain hunting, check the Transport for London website (www.tfl.gov.uk) and be prepared to do some research. If you just want convenience and unlimited travel, purchase the appropriate Travelcard or Oyster card before you go.

Are the buses and subways safe? Most of the system usually *feels* safe. Pickpockets and beggars can be a problem at times in Tube stations and larger security threats are taken very seriously. Based on personal experience, evacuating a rail station because of a bomb threat is no laughing matter. Those are rare exceptions and the Tube is generally a safe, dependable way to get around London.

Here are some tips for safer Tube travel:

- Get a good Transport for London map and plan your Tube journey before you go. Don't wander around looking like a lost tourist and an easy mark.

- Use a travel wallet to keep your money out of sight. Sure, it is awkward to dig under your shirt or jacket every time you need money, but it foils pickpockets.

- Don't leave any bags or packages sitting unattended. The security police may suspect a bomb and blow up your bag of souvenirs!

- Have one adult quickly distribute tickets/passes just before boarding a bus or going through the Tube ticket turnstiles. Then collect them again and put them in a safe place. If you lose a card, you are out of luck.

- Touch-in Oyster cards on the yellow readers in the station and touch-out when you leave the station at your destination.

- Hold children's hands.

- Mind the gap! Our favorite Transport for London phrase, this refers to the gap between the train and the platform at some Tube stops.

- Look for the electronic signs on platforms that tell you how long until the next train arrives and where it is heading. The signs display the final stop of the next train.

Changing between different Underground lines in a station can often involve a very long walk through connecting passageways. Also, with passageways, stairs, and escalators in Underground stations, it is sometimes quicker to walk short distances on London streets rather than take a short ride on the Tube.

The advantage to bus travel is that you can sightsee while commuting around London. The disadvantage is that buses creep along busy streets during rush hours at a pace almost slower than walking. There are a huge number of bus routes in central London and the maps and route/schedule information posted at each bus stop can be confusing.

Consult the online journey planner on the Transport for London website at www.tfl.gov.uk. Keep in mind that buses generally only stop at marked stops. There are automatic stops and "request" stops where you must hail a bus to get on, or indicate that you want to get off. Special night bus routes operate overnight and provide public transportation when the Tube is closed and taxis are scarce.

Taxi!

> The driver looked hard at Paddington and then at the inside of his nice, clean taxi. "Bears is sixpence extra," he said, gruffly … "
>
> —from *A Bear Called Paddington* by Michael Bond

The black London taxi is as much a symbol of the city as Tower Bridge or Big Ben. In recent years, the traditional black color is often replaced by garish advertising painted on the cabs. Waiting in the taxi queue, we suspect most parents hope to get into a traditional black taxicab while their kids root for the cab painted like a newspaper or done up in retro-psychedelic colors.

No matter what the color, a real London taxi is a reliable, if expensive, way to get to your destination. Unlike some U.S. cities where almost anyone with a driver's license can operate a cab, London requires taxi drivers to acquire *the knowledge*—a detailed understanding of London's streets and sights. The knowledge means that when you tell the driver your destination is the "Hotel Expensif" you won't get a blank look (unless the driver can't understand your American accent). London taxi drivers know where you're going.

Arriving after a long plane journey, a ride in a taxi may be your first impression of London. Jet-lagged kids wake up fast when they ride in the taxi's rear-facing jump seats, hang on for dear life, and realize WE'RE DRIVING ON THE WRONG SIDE OF THE ROAD!

London has other taxi-like conveyances. Order a taxi from your hotel and you'll probably get a private car service or minicab. Be aware that the training of the driver and condition of the vehicle can vary by car company. Minicabs cannot pick up passengers on the street; you have to telephone a minicab company to arrange a ride.

A word about costs. London's official taxicabs use a metering system that records time and distance traveled. Minicabs are freer to charge what they like; some use meters, but most have set fees. So the laws of economics apply, one of which is "It's easy to take money from tourists." In a taxicab, be wary of the few drivers who will deliberately take longer-than-necessary routes, sometimes with an excuse of avoiding traffic jams or roadwork. In a taxi or minicab, get an estimated fare before you start your journey. If you are traveling with lots of luggage, make sure the taxi can carry it all. While official London taxis can fit a couple of big suitcases in the boot (trunk) and a bag or two in the front compartment next to the driver, minicabs may have more limited space for baggage.

Finally, one other potential hazard is the so-called taxi "tout." Working airports and rail stations, these guys pounce on tourists, carry bags to a car outside, and promise low fares. Two problems: the fares are usually not lower and the practice of touting is illegal.

Telephones And The Internet

It wasn't often that Paddington made a telephone call—for one thing he always found it a bit difficult with paws ...

—from *Paddington Goes to Town* by Michael Bond

Phone Number Formats

Telephone listings in British publications don't always follow a consistent format, so we've standardized most of the telephone numbers in this book using the following formats.

London phone numbers are 11 digits long:

020 7123 4567

The 8 digit phone number, usually starting with 7 or 8 for London
The area/city code—London is 020

But you don't always dial all 11 digits:

- From outside the United Kingdom, drop the first zero, but add the 011 international access code followed by 44 (the United Kingdom country code).

- Within greater London, drop the 020 city code.

Outside of London and/or for certain toll-free or *national rate* numbers, the 11 digits are split up a bit differently. All have a leading zero, then a geographical code that's between two and five digits, followed by the rest of the number. Strangely enough, a phone number does not have to total 11 digits in less populated areas. Consistency is not part of the vernacular in British telephone listings. We've seen phone numbers listed like this:

0207-123 4567

(0) 207 123 4567

(020) 7123 4567

(0) 20 7123 4567

(440) 20-7123 4567

Be prepared to be confused!

Other Important Numbers

- Dial 999 or 112 for emergency fire, police, and ambulance services.
- Dial 101 (where available) for non-emergency public safety services.
- Dial 100 for operator assistance.
- Directory assistance numbers vary by telephone company, but all begin with 118.
- Cell phones start with 07 followed by nine digits.
- Toll-free numbers start with 0800 or 0808 and generally cannot be reached from outside the U.K.

- Other numbers starting with 08 are not free, but they are usually a low national per minute rate. The national rate numbers often cannot be called from outside the U.K. either.

- Numbers starting with 09 are premium calls—some of which we can't discuss in a family travel guidebook!

Calling Britain

To call Britain from the U.S. or other countries:

- Dial the international access code (011).
- Then dial the United Kingdom country code (44).
- Do not dial the zero prefix on the British telephone number.
- Then dial the rest of the phone number (for example: 20 7123 4567).

Phoning Home

To call the United States or Canada from Britain:

- Dial the international access code (00).
- Next dial the U.S./Canada country code (1).
- Then the area code and phone number (for example: 555 992-1234).

Most hotels add an outrageous surcharge to outgoing calls. Your own long distance carrier at home may have a toll-free access number that you can dial directly from overseas. This allows you to use a calling card and pay lower rates for international calls. Competition continues to change the face of international communications, so you may find any number of low cost ways to phone home. These include pre-paid calling cards, international "call back" systems, mobile phones, and internet telephone services.

Pay Phones

Pay phones in London come in several varieties. While there are still coin operated pay phones in some places, many pay phones take only credit cards or phone cards. The prepaid phone cards can be purchased from shops all over the city. Authorities fight a losing battle with escort services and others who continually post pornographic advertisements in many central London phone booths. Use caution before letting young children into a phone booth.

Mobile Phones

Cell phones, or *mobiles* in Britspeak, are the communications device of choice for a huge number of London residents. For a visitor, however, taking and using a cell phone in a foreign country requires a bit of planning. Not all North American cell phones will operate in Britain without some adjustments to hardware and/or service agreements. The cell phone industry changes constantly and today's best advice is outdated almost as soon as it is written. But in general, here are some options for cell phone service:

Some North American cell phone providers offer worldwide, or country-specific, roaming for existing phones. You can usually activate this service to coincide with your trip, although there may be a minimum service period of a month or longer.

You can rent an international cell phone and take it on your trip. Companies that rent phones express deliver them before you depart. Upon return, you ship the phone back. This arrangement works, although you do have the hassle and cost of receiving and returning the phone. But cell phone equipment has become so cheap that buying an international phone can be as economical as renting. There are a number of companies that specialize in sale of international cell phones, usually along with providing airtime and a billing service. Like rentals, these phones are delivered before your trip, but the phone is yours to keep and perhaps use on a subsequent visit.

One of the better options is to buy a used or inexpensive cell phone that is capable of operating in the United Kingdom, then purchase a SIM card from a communications store once you arrive in London. SIMs can be purchased with varying minutes of usage pre-loaded. The downside to purchasing a SIM after arrival is that you won't know your cell phone number before your trip begins, thus making it hard to use as an emergency contact for folks back home. Finally, another option is to buy a phone and service package from one of many mobile phone companies in the United Kingdom.

Voice Over Internet

Taking a laptop computer on your trip? Use it to phone home. Voice Over Internet Protocol (VOIP) services allow computer users to call over the internet, both to other computers and to regular telephones. Calls between computers are often free.

Websites

Most British web addresses on the internet look like this:

http://www.terrifictourbook.co.uk

In this book we have not shown the *http://* unless the rest of the address is something other than *www*. For these oddball addresses, we've shown the whole thing, including the *http://* to avoid any confusion.

Web sites change faster than the weather in London, so please forgive any expired addresses we have listed. Because webmasters often tinker around with individual pages on a website, we have avoided going too far down the website file pathways when listing web addresses. This means we may show www.royal.gov.uk as the address for royal palace information when the actual page was, at last check, www.royal.gov.uk/output/Page553.asp.

By the way, the *Let's Take the Kids to London* website is:

www.KidsToLondon.com

Medical And Money Matters

Is There A Doctor In The House?

This is a subject that most people would rather not think about—getting sick while on your long-planned vacation to London. But these things happen, and a little preparedness goes a long way. Before you leave home, check with your health insurance provider and find out exactly what coverage your family will have while traveling abroad. If this coverage information is not already available in medical plan documents you have on hand, get it in writing from the insurer.

Many insurers will reimburse for emergency medical expenses abroad, but they may require you to contact them for authorization. Managed care plans (HMOs and similar plans) can be real sticklers about notification. Your medical insurance card is probably useless in Britain, but take it anyway, especially if it includes the phone numbers you must call to notify the insurer of a medical emergency. Notice that we said most insurers will *reimburse* emergency medical expenses. This still means you would have to pay doctors, pharmacy, or hospital bills directly in Britain.

The United Kingdom operates a nationalized health insurance plan and anyone, even a tourist, can obtain emergency medical treatment through this plan. Anything more than emergency treatment is provided on a fee for service basis.

If this medical insurance situation makes you uneasy, then consider purchasing separate travelers' health insurance through a reputable travel agency or insurance company. There are many plans available, some of which can be combined with coverage for lost baggage, travel delays, and other vacation disasters.

What should you do if you have a non-life threatening medical problem in London? Maybe a child comes down with an ear infection. (Can you tell a parent wrote this?) Here are some sources of medical help for visitors:

- There are private walk-in medical clinics catering to tourists, such as MediCentre located in Victoria, Euston, and Waterloo rail stations and other central London locations.

- Call the front desk of your hotel. Most large hotels have on-call physicians or arrangements with medical centers, but this service can be expensive.

- Many London hospitals operate walk-in centers, minor injury units and/or accident/emergency departments.

- In an emergency, telephone 999 for ambulance services.

One other tactic used by traveling families is to pack a fairly extensive medicine kit for overseas travel. Sometimes just carrying this kit acts like a talisman to keep illness at bay. If someone in your family has a history of illness, be sure to check with a physician before you leave to determine appropriate medicines to take with you. Have the generic names of any prescription medicines, since brand names may be different outside North America. Prescriptions are filled by *chemists* in England.

Money Matters (Boy, Does It!)

For inside his hat was not just one, but a whole pile of coins. There were so many, in fact, that the latest addition—whatever it had been—was lost for all time amongst a vast assortment of pennies, threepenny pieces, sixpences; coins of so many different shapes, sizes and values that Paddington soon gave up trying to count them all.

—from *Paddington Goes to Town* by Michael Bond

You've probably already concluded that your trip to London is going to cost you a bundle. How big a bundle is something over which you have *some* control, but regardless, a family traveling to London needs a fair amount of money in British currency/cash, credit cards, ATM cards, or some combination of these.

For the moment, the basic unit of currency in England is the Pound Sterling. Great Britain may adopt the Euro (the official currency of the European Union), but for now the British pound still rules. The pound (£) is divided into 100 pence (p) and the following are common British currency denominations:

Bills	Coins	
£5	1 pence	20 pence
£10	2 pence	50 pence
£20	5 pence	£1
£50	10 pence	£2

For many years, Britain operated a complex, non-decimal system of currency. While the old system is gone, it is still easy for a tourist to get confused because the pound is also referred to as *Sterling* and, more colloquially, a pound is a *quid*.

Making Change

Fumbling with unfamiliar bills and coins can ruin your image as a savvy tourist, so become familiar with the look and feel of pounds and pence before you start spending them. Learning about British coins can be an educational game, so try to obtain some coins before the trip and let your children play with them.

Foreign currency looks so different to the American eye that spending it sometimes doesn't seem real. We call this the "Monopoly money" syndrome. Maybe this is a good thing since overseas travel can be so expensive and, for some people, thinking about the cost can almost ruin the trip. But if you don't want to go bankrupt, learn the currency and make a mental conversion to dollars when spending pounds.

Whack-A-Mole Currency Rip Offs

If there is one lesson to be learned about money and your trip, it is this: many banks, credit card companies, travelers check companies, debit card issuers, airport money exchanges, and the like, are out to rip you off. They do this by imposing fees—sometimes deliberately hidden fees—on foreign currency transactions. So, if your local bank says "We can get British Pounds for you, in any amount, for just a $7 fee," they are forgetting to tell you "But our exchange rate is about six percent worse than what you can get from an ATM once you arrive in London." If your credit card company says "Your card is good at thousands of places in the UK," they're forgetting to add "For a fee of four percent on each purchase." If your bank says "Sure your VISA debit card is good at ATMs in London," they have left out "At the currency exchange rates set by VISA." And if your otherwise trustworthy local AAA Travel Office offers to sell you a convenient "tip pack" in British Pounds, watch out, their markup can be outrageous.

But wait, there's more. Say you take your trusty credit card to Britain, a card that charges a four percent foreign transaction fee, and you decide to use it to rent a car. The car rental company offers to charge the transaction directly to your card in dollars, instead of pounds, for your convenience. Or sometimes, they don't offer this option, they just go ahead and do it. This is called dynamic currency conversion. Terrific, you think, if they charge the card in dollars there won't be a currency conversion fee added by the credit card company. That may be true, but the rate that the car rental company used to charge your card in dollars also included a currency conversion fee added by the local dynamic conversion service instead of your credit card company. Oh, and what's worse, since the transaction is still considered "foreign" your credit card company could go ahead and add its own fee to the transaction.

With all these potential traps, what can a traveler do? Keep reading for some hints, but keep in mind that this is a very fluid area and today's best advice could easily change as new fees are imposed.

ATM Cards

Most people routinely use automatic teller machines to get cash at home and there is no reason to stop using ATMs when traveling to London. ATMs are known as *cash points* in Britain. Before you go, check with your bank to make sure that your ATM card and personal identification number (PIN) will work overseas—four digit numeric PINs are most common abroad. Many foreign ATMs allow access to your checking account only, so don't count on being able to transfer funds between savings and checking.

Be wary of ATM cards with a credit card logo on the front. Some of these add the credit card company's foreign transaction fees when you use an overseas ATM. You can get a "plain vanilla" ATM card, without credit company logo (and fees), from many U.S. banks and credit unions.

Convenience is a big factor for using ATMs, but the other great thing about using your ATM card in London is that you usually get the best possible exchange rates. Be sure to use fee-free ATMs in London. Normally, ATMs associated with major British banks do not charge a user fee, but machines in pubs, convenience stores, and other areas may impose a fee. Your own bank will probably charge a small fee each time you use an ATM in London. In this case, it is wise to make fewer, larger transactions, rather than repeatedly hitting ATMs for £20 pounds at a time. Some U.S. banks do not charge transaction fees and some have affiliations with British banks that allow customers fee-free ATM use.

Credit Cards

Plastic is just as fantastic in London as it is at home. VISA and Mastercard are widely accepted in London and credit card transactions are usually converted from pounds to dollars at favorable exchange rates. Rather than the retail rate, which you might get at one of those currency exchange booths at the airport, credit card companies use a better commercial rate to convert your charges in British pounds to American dollars.

Many credit card issuers have added overseas transaction fees, either to gouge travelers (our view) or to compensate for the added cost of doing business abroad (the credit companies' view). Fortunately, you should still be able to find credit cards without these fees, but you may have to shop around to get a fee-free card in advance of your trip. VISA and Mastercard International corporations add a small percentage fee for all foreign transactions. There is no escaping this fee. But the credit card issuer—the bank or credit union that sent you the card—can also add another currency conversion/overseas transaction fee. Check with your bank and if they have this fee, find another credit card that does not. Possibilities include certain cards issued by USAA Savings Bank and some credit unions.

We warned earlier about dynamic currency conversion. How can you avoid this trap? Refuse to sign any credit card receipt overseas that is not charged in the local currency. Just send it back and say "Charge it in pounds." Some merchants may plead ignorance or claim that their credit card systems automatically change the currency. That's not cricket, so play hardball here. The merchants' agreements with your credit card company probably *require* them to offer you the choice of paying in local currency.

One final credit card caution. Before you leave home, contact the customer service department of your credit card company and inform them that you will be traveling overseas. The reason? Credit card companies watch transactions accumulating on your card. If these go from *Wal-Mart $13.99, The Gap $29.95 ...* to *Harrods £50, Fortnum & Mason £100 ...* the card issuer may suspect that someone has stolen your card and gone on a London shopping spree and then block further use of the card.

Travelers Checks

Travelers checks have become monetary dinosaurs, largely replaced by the plastic convenience of credit and ATM cards. For most travelers, there is no reason to buy travelers checks, or the newer travelers check cards. Travelers checks include currency conversion fees, either when issued, when cashed, or both. But travelers checks issued in British pounds at least mean you can use them directly in London without having to cash and convert them into local currency. This is a big convenience and we strongly recommend taking pound travelers checks if you choose to use travelers checks. Be aware that not every merchant in London will accept pound travelers checks and you may pay a fee to cash them at banks, post offices, or other locations in London. Travelers check cards are more widely accepted. Almost no London merchants will accept dollar travelers checks. If they do, you'll be hit with fees, sometimes hidden in unfavorable currency exchange rates.

Travelers checks do retain one valuable feature—they can be replaced if lost or stolen. In addition, in the rare event that your ATM and/or credit cards don't work at some point on your trip, travelers checks can be a backup source of funds.

Exchange Rate Roulette

The value of the British pound fluctuates against the U.S. dollar, so it pays to keep an eye on foreign exchange rates. If you think that the value of the dollar will decline by the time you take your trip, consider pre-paying some of your trip costs such as car rental, hotel, and rail tickets. On the other hand, if you believe the value of the dollar will go up, don't pre-pay trip costs. Just wait and use ATM cards and credit cards when you reach London. Another strategy is to just ignore the currency markets and enjoy your trip. This is especially true after arriving in London because you have no control over the international monetary market, so why sweat it?

Dash Cash

After spending long hours on a plane, claiming luggage, clearing customs and immigration, and finding your way through an unfamiliar airport, the last thing many people want to do is search for a place to exchange money before starting a vacation. One way to avoid this extra hassle by taking a small amount of British currency with you. Some travel agencies and banks sell foreign currency and you can purchase currency online as well. Keep in mind that this is an expensive way to obtain pounds compared to using the ATMs located in the arrivals areas of London airports.

That Nasty VAT—Valued Added Tax

Many Americans are used to paying sales tax when they shop and they readily accept a four or five percent nuisance tax added to the ticketed price. It comes as quite a shock to learn that you're paying a 17.5% Value Added Tax (VAT) when you rent a hotel room, buy a gift, eat dinner, or rent a car in Britain.

Most quoted prices in Britain include the VAT. That's one reason some things look really expensive in London; the other reason is that many things *are* really expensive. You can get a refund of the VAT on some purchases, but you have to spend a lot in one store, do some paperwork, and go through an extra customs line at the airport when you leave Britain. If you go into a London store and make a sizable purchase, the store may help you get a VAT refund. Be sure to ask if the store has a VAT refund procedure. There are several competing companies, but the most common is Global Refund (www.globalrefund.com). There is a fee for this service.

A couple of provisos. If you're traveling on to another European Union country, wait until you finally leave for home before getting the goods inspected by that country's customs agents. Unless you are a business traveler, you can't recover the VAT you shelled out on hotels, meals, car rental, etc. For tourists, this part of the VAT is an unavoidable cost of traveling in the European Union.

Good luck. It takes some work to save money this way. Many people don't bother with it, especially if they're not buying a lot of merchandise.

Britspeak

Skip To The Loo

The wise parent of young children is always bathroom-aware. Traveling to Britain presents some special challenges, not the least of which is that the locals don't even call it a "bathroom." In Britain, bathrooms are strictly rooms where you take a bath. Here are some of the Britspeak terms that do apply:

- Loo
- WC
- Necessary
- Gents
- Ladies
- Nappy changing room (for babies)
- Toilet (can't argue that one)
- In one restaurant the signs read Elton John and Olivia Newton John in a musical, if dated, theme.

Finding a public restroom is not too difficult in London, but don't go in unless you are carrying a 20 pence coin. Although some public toilets no longer charge admission, many still do. Our children described the public toilet fee as "20p to pee." Restrooms are also available in larger

restaurants, hotel lobbies, museums, department stores, and other locations. If you look respectable, no one objects if you use these facilities,
and they are often cleaner than public restrooms.

More Britspeak

For Americans, one great thing about going to England is that the
people there speak our language. Well, not exactly. We've used the term
Britspeak to refer to some of the obvious differences between American
"English" and the language spoken by most of the inhabitants of
London. Here are a few Britspeak definitions:

What they say	What they mean
Aubergine	Eggplant
Bill	Check (at a restaurant)
Biscuits	Cookies
Bobby	Police officer
Bonnet	Car hood
Boot	Car trunk
Cash point	Automated teller machine (ATM)
Chemist shop	Drug store, pharmacy
Chips	French fries
Clotted cream	A thick, sweet cream used as a teatime spread for bread or scones
Coach	Bus
Crisps	Potato chips
Cuppa	Cup of tea
Devonshire cream	Almost the same as clotted cream
En suite	Private bath (in a hotel room)
First floor	Second floor
Flat	Apartment
Football	Soccer
Fortnight	Two weeks
Give way	Yield
Ground floor	First floor

Iced lolly	Popsicle
Jelly	Jell-O
Lay-by	Roadside parking pull-off area
Licensed	Restaurant with a liquor license
Lift	Elevator
Lorry	Truck
Maize	Corn
Nappy	Diaper
Plaice	Flounder (fish)
Pasty	Pastry turnover filled with vegetables and/or meat
Petrol	Gasoline, *expensive* gasoline
Porridge	Oatmeal
Post-box	Mailbox
Pram	Baby carriage
Priority	Right of way
Pudding	Dessert
Pushchair	Baby stroller
Queue	Line at a store, theater, or bus stop. Standing in queues is a national pastime in Britain.
Quid	A pound (£)
Roundabout	Traffic circle
Scheme	Plan or program ("scheme" does not have a negative connotation)
Scone	A pastry. A sweet biscuit on which you pile clotted creme and jam at teatime. Only fattening if you think about it.
Serviette	Napkin
Sterling	Pounds, money
Subway	Pedestrian underpass tunnel
Surgery	A doctor's or dentist's office
Take-away	Carry out food
Tube	Subway
Underground	Subway
Way out	Exit
Zebra crossing	Pedestrian crossing (except at the zoo)

Tick-Tock

Although the clock face of Big Ben shows only the familiar 12 hours, Britain officially uses a 24-hour time system. "Officially" does not mean "uniformly" and Londoners are as likely to say *3:00 p.m.* as they are say *1500*. Morning hours are easy—0800 is 8:00 a.m. When confronted with unfamiliar afternoon times, just remember to subtract 12. So 1500 minus 1200 equals 3:00 p.m. Got that? If not, here's a conversion chart:

The hands on Big Ben say...	Officially, it is ...
12:00 (midnight)	2400
1:00 a.m.	0100
2:00 a.m.	0200
and so on until we get to the "weirder" afternoon hours...	
12:00 (noon)	1200
1:00 p.m.	1300
2:00 p.m.	1400
3:00 p.m.	1500
4:00 p.m.	1600
5:00 p.m.	1700
6:00 p.m.	1800
7:00 p.m.	1900
8:00 p.m.	2000
9:00 p.m.	2100
10:00 p.m.	2200
11:00 p.m.	2300

Time To Leave

No matter how long and fascinating your visit to London, eventually it's time to leave. How do you know for sure? If you're a savvy tourist, one who tries to blend in with the local scene, it may be time to depart when other tourists ask *you* for directions. Standing on a footbridge in St. James's Park, I was approached by an American tourist (a person whose regional accent was unmistakable):

> "What's that building over there?" he asked.
> "Buckingham Palace" I replied, trying to hide my incredulity.
> "Oh REALLY?" he said.

Yep, it is *definitely* time to leave when fellow tourists mistake you for a local!

Back in the U.S. after 15 days in Britain, our family unloaded piles of dirty laundry, then sat down to our first meal since our return home. Our son remarked "I can't believe it. Last night we were having dinner at a pub in London. Today we're back at our kitchen table." That, son, is the magic of overseas jet travel. And it's the reason you know we'll go back.

About the Author

David White is the budget director for a top-rated public school system in Maryland. Although well-versed in local government and politics, as author of *Let's Take The Kids To London*, David White has two key qualifications:

- he is the father of two
- he has happily taken the kids to London many times

Index

A

B

G

P

Q

T

978-0-595-13953-8
0-595-13953-1

Made in the USA